MEET THE WITNESSES

OF THE MIRACLE OF THE SUN

by

John M. Haffert

THE AMERICAN SOCIETY FOR THE DEFENSE
OF TRADITION, FAMILY AND PROPERTY — TFP

SPRING GROVE, PENN. 17362

Cover illustration: Picture of the crowd at the Cova da Iria during the
Miracle of the Sun, October 13, 1917.

ISBN-13: 978-1-877905-35-3
ISBN-10: 1-877905-35-6
Library of Congress Control Number: 2006924932

Printed in the United States of America

Imprimatur:
Most Rev. John Venancio, S.T.D., Bishop of Leiria

The author has done all possible to guarantee the absolute accuracy of all contained in this book which has been rewritten several times, with manuscripts submitted on each occasion to most competent critics.

Greatest debt is acknowledged to Maria de Freitaz, celebrated Portuguese writer and International Secretary of the Blue Army, for carrying through the bulk of the research work, and to Rev. Messias Coelho, Professor at the Seminary in Fundao, Portugal.

Most of the photographs in this book are original, but for some of the 1917 photographs acknowledgement is made to Gilbert Renault, author of *Fatima, Esperance du Monde,* and to his publishers, Librairie Plon, Paris, France.

Special appreciation is also due to the author's esteemed friend, the Very Reverend Canon Galamba da Oliveira, one of Portugal's greatest preachers and writers and perhaps the world's most outstanding authority on the message of Fatima, for his work on the manuscript. And thanks to all the hundreds of persons... witnesses of the miracle... who collaborated so generously.

This book is dedicated to Most Reverend José Correia da Silva, D.D., Sister Mary of the Immaculate Heart, D.C., Francisco and Jacinta Marto and Dona Maria de Freitas.

Letter from the Bishop of Fatima

My dear Mr. Haffert,

You ask a few words for your new book on Fatima, *Meet the Witnesses*, the manuscript of which I have just read and by which I was enchanted.

Forgive me for not having time or competence for a lengthy and profound introduction such as you and the readers of this book would merit and naturally expect from the Bishop of Fatima... But I wish to congratulate you on this book which is truly new in the vast bibliography of Fatima. I am certain that it is going to do much for souls seeking light on a theme so real.

I profit by this occasion to congratulate you, once more, and to express my gratitude for the heroic perseverance with which, for so many years, you have devoted yourself to the diffusion, propaganda, and clarification of the message of Fatima in the United States and throughout the world.

And continue! Our Lady will not fail to help you nor to obtain for you a great reward. For this I pray: That the Most Holy Virgin reward you with most abundant blessings, for yourself, your family, and for the labors and magnificent work to which you have consecrated your life.

I recommend myself to your prayers, and to those of your friends, as I remain,

Very devotedly yours in the Sacred Hearts of Jesus and Mary,

Most Rev. John Venancio
Bishop of Leiria

&❧ CONTENTS ℭℰ

FOREWORD I

My worry, when I opened the manuscript of this book with the view of writing a foreword, was that I was going to have to say something good about it whether I thought it was good or not.

What was the author going to say? What could be the interest of another book on Fatima?

But as I progressed in reading, light streamed from these pages as through a thick fog through which the sun dashes its beams. I came to know clearly, definitely, what this foreword would be.

Years ago it was easy to write a book on Fatima, and almost any book on the subject was sure of some success. The world wanted to know the story.

But today? Would it not be presumptuous for any writer to seek to add to the vast number of books, not a few of which have been written by some of the best writers of our times... all on the same subject? It would appear certain that Fatima will fill one of the greatest niches in the Marian bibliography of all time, so many are the books on this subject. Yet who would have thought so some four decades ago, when there appeared those first small books: *The Miraculous Cloud of Smoke, The Events of Fatima, The Wonderful Episodes of Fatima*. Yet hundreds of pamphlets and books, on every aspect of Fatima, have been added in the ensuing forty years.

All the books we have read on Fatima differ... in intrinsic value, literary brilliance, historical accuracy, sincerity of expression. We can say, without fear of contradiction, that the number of constructive books on Fatima is incomparably greater than bad and destructive ones, and that there was no detail not the object of study, by some writer or other, until this book.

The bibliography of Fatima is truly enriched by *Meet the Witnesses*.

It is not a book of mysticism or theology. Neither is it a romance. But it holds our interest like a novel or the report of a remarkable *cause celebre*.

This report of events happening in 1917 has the freshness of a news report, using depositions of living witnesses, eye witnesses to the great event. Enormous interest develops page after page.

The author looked for and found a certain number of persons who witnessed the miraculous event which the children of Fatima had foretold would take place at a certain time, in a certain place. He heard them, recorded their testimony, and publishes this testimony in their own words, without consideration of their social level or degree of education.

This book, *Meet the Witnesses*, is a challenge to today's incredulity as the very fact it describes is a challenge from undeniable facts, seen by thousands of witnesses (from whom the author presents many). Let the reader judge, and at the same time judge himself. If he is honest, if he is sincere, if he is dedicated to truth which brings freedom, let him come to the challenge after reading these pages and deny the facts if he dares.

John Haffert, accustomed to handle a pen easily and adroitly, has put himself at the service of truth throughout his life... a life still in bloom, but already filled with ripe fruit. All America knows him and it is not up to me to introduce him, as he needs no introduction. He may sometimes be the subject of discussion, even of attack, and like all men... he may err. But he is sufficiently humble to confess an error and correct it. And like a rock beaten by waves, at each attack John Haffert has remained more steadfast, more brilliant and glorious. If there were nothing else to bring him the honor of these words, there are three jewels of inestimable value which will immortalize his name in the noble gallery of illustrious lay Catholics of the United States of our age: His profound devotion to the Mother of God and to Holy Mother Church; the initiative of the great pilgrimage of the statue of Our Lady of Fatima (the Pilgrim Virgin) through Canada and the United States since October, 1947; and finally, that powerful and enthusiastic crusade of the Blue Army, which has spread through the entire world to bring to all mankind the message and devotion of Our Lady of Fatima.

But this book, *Meet the Witnesses*, is another jewel. It will bring to all devotees of Our Lady, and to all the scholars of Fatima, a deep joy, an enormous satisfaction. This alone causes me to thank John Haffert for his friendship and for the honor of writing this preface, for the magnificent opportunity of paying homage... in truth and at ease... to the real value of this work and to the talent of an author of such size.

> *Leiria, Portugal*
> *July 13, 1961*
> *V. Rev. Canon Galamba de Oliveira, D.D.*

Publisher's note: Canon Galamba de Oliveira, writer of this preface, is author of several books and one of the most celebrated writers and preachers of Portugal. He is perhaps the world's greatest living authority on Fatima, having held a position of authority under two successive Bishops in Fatima's continuing process of ecclesiastical investigations.

FOREWORD II

When Sister Lucia died on February 13, 2005, thousands flocked to the Carmelite convent in Coimbra to pray before the remains of the last of the three Fatima seers.

For decades, Sister Lucia, a cloistered nun, inaccessible to most of the world, by her presence within the convent walls had reminded millions of Fatima and Our Lady's requests: that we pray the Rosary daily, offer penance for the conversion of sinners, abandon sin, do the Five First Saturdays devotion and other acts of reparation for the offenses committed against her Immaculate Heart. The Blessed Mother had also warned of a chastisement if her requests were not heeded.

While so rich in meaning, Fatima is also so easy to understand. I once heard it compared to what happens at times in family life. The comparison was made by Prof. Plinio Corrêa de Oliveira, founder of the Brazilian Society for the Defense of Tradition, Family and Property (TFP) and inspirer of the other autonomous sister TFPs around the world.

He used the image of a father who is upset at the misbehavior of his children and is ready to chastise them unless they change. To encourage them to change, he asks the mother to warn the children of his intention. Hopefully her words will suffice to convince them to improve and no punishment will be needed. She gathers the children around her and speaks to them as only mothers can. In a sense, this is what Our Lady did at Fatima.

But have we reformed our lives? Will we have to be chastised before we change? We need only consider the general decline of morals since 1917 to realize that the world has not heeded Our Lady's maternal call to conversion.

In these days following the death of Sister Lucia, we would do well to think back to October 13, 1917. Three months earlier Our Lady had promised Lucia a miracle "so that all might see and believe." The news had spread throughout Portugal, and over 70,000 people traveled to the Cova da Iria to witness the miracle.

Atheists and probably even some Catholics ridiculed the "credulous," "gullible" pilgrims. However, Our Lady did work a miracle. And while some believers may have expected a miracle like the wonderful cures at Lourdes, Our Lady astonished the crowd with a miracle so terrifying that many thought the end of the world had come.

Professor de Oliveira himself wondered if the Miracle of the Sun might not indicate the magnitude of the chastisement an unrepentant mankind was bringing on itself. The sun had unexpectedly spun all over the sky. Might other things we normally take for granted "spiral" out of control and threaten us with total destruction?

To encourage us, then, to reflect on this miracle, America Needs Fatima is reprinting *Meet the Witnesses*, written in 1960 by John M. Haffert, co-founder of the Blue Army. Mr. Haffert's love and dedication led him to seek out many who had been at the Cova da Iria on the day of this historic miracle. He published their invaluable testimony in *Meet the Witnesses.*

This is a book that could not be written today, for most of the eyewitnesses he interviewed, like Sister Lucia, have been called by God. By recording their words, Mr. Haffert rendered a great and enduring service to the Church. Those who benefit from reading them will be indebted to Mr. Haffert.

These personal accounts bring the Miracle of the Sun to life. They allow us to picture vividly the sun spinning in the sky and nearly crashing to earth. As we read on, we echo the cry of the witnesses. In the depths of our souls, we too exclaim, "We believe!"

Mr. Haffert's compelling work invites us to prepare diligently for serious trials in a world that deserves divine punishment. *Meet the Witnesses* challenges us to strengthen our faith, increase our love, and proclaim our unshakeable certainty in

Mary's promise: "Finally, My Immaculate Heart will triumph!"

Raymond E. Drake
March 10, 2006

PREFACE

In the case of the miracle described in this book, the "official" description of the miracle was written by unbelievers and first published in a neutral press.

The "miracle" primarily conveyed the impression, to over one hundred thousand witnesses, that the world was about to end. And at a predicted time and place, a phenomenon occurred which could not be explained by natural laws.

A light was seen in the sky which looked like the sun. It was visible within a radius of more than twenty miles, clearly defined (hence not something seen through a fog or mist), whirled in the sky like a wheel of fire, threw off shafts of colored light which colored objects on the ground. After several minutes, it seemed suddenly to loose itself from the sky and to plummet toward the earth, causing the crowd to believe that the world was about to end. It was over in twelve minutes.

Three months in advance, three children had predicted that a miracle would take place, on that spot, at that particular time, "so that everyone would believe" in a message which they had received from Heaven.

So here we have a modern wonder, outside of nature, explicitly ascribed to God, as proof of future events in the world including war to come to the world from Russia.

From this brief description one gets very little of the impact of what happened.

Miracles—by the very fact that they are miracles—seem unreal.

But on our belief in this miracle—and on our reaction to it—probably depends the avoidance of atomic war. That is why this book is written.

For those who may not understand the nature of a "miracle," a brief word:

Childbirth may be a "miracle" to some. To others flying saucers may be "miracles." But a miracle in the true sense of the word is a wonderful event above, contrary to, outside nature.

Examples of miracles "above nature" are the raising of Lazarus to life (John XI), or the restoration of life to the dead son of the widow of Naim. Examples of miracles "outside nature" are the multiplication of the loaves and fishes (John VI), or the changing of the water into wine at Cana (John II). And, finally, a miracle "contrary to nature" is the preservation of the three children in the fiery furnace (Daniel 111).

In its simplest terms, a miracle is something to the senses that is out of the ordinary. St. Thomas Aquinas teaches: "Those effects are rightly to be termed miracles which are wrought by Divine power apart from the order usually observed in nature" (Contra Gent. III cii).

In scripture miracles are called "the Finger of God" (Exodus VIII, 19; Luke XI, 20), the "Hand of the Lord" (1st Kings V6), the "Hand of Our God" (I Esdres, VIII 31).

It is important in understanding the nature of a miracle to understand that natural means may be used in the miracle, but what is produced has an utter lack of proportion to the effect normally expected. We have a specific example of this in the miracle about which this book is written.

When an event takes place which is above, contrary to, or outside the nature of those known laws, as a sign of some special mission or gift and explicitly ascribed to God, then we call it truly a "miracle."

Chapter 1
EYE WITNESS

Immediately after World War II, two American writers were invited to Portugal to review the "miracle"... which was then beginning to attract world attention... and even given the special privilege of talking freely with the only living one of the three children who had predicted the "miracle" and had transmitted the message and prophecies.

One writer was Dr. William Thomas Walsh, who wrote an excellent and quite typical book titled *Our Lady of Fatima* (Published by Macmillan, it had a wide circulation, particularly when reissued as a paperback).

The other writer was too stunned by what he witnessed at Fatima. How could he put into words, no matter how well chosen, the look in the eyes of witnesses? How could he speak matter-of-factly in view of the events which had now whirled mankind to the brink of atomic war? How could he convey the *fact* of what he saw and experienced at Fatima when in himself the dawn of realization... there in the presence of eyewitnesses, on the spot where it happened... was a shock, inexplicable and ineffable?

Dr. Walsh had done all that any writer could be expected to do: He had objectively, clearly, authoritatively recounted what happened. And who could cross the chasm between mere believing that such a thing might have happened, and *the actual realization that it did, except the witnesses themselves?*

Yet this is what the world... or at least enough persons in the world... are expected to do. They are expected to react to this "miracle" not as an historical event, but as a crucial reaching of the Hand of God into the hearts of a frightened humanity.

Good persons of various faiths have gone to Fatima and there... in the presence of the reality, and particularly after talking to witnesses... have crossed that psychological chasm between knowing and realizing.

Meanwhile dozens of books have appeared in dozens of nations telling the same facts... mysterious, marvelous, difficult to believe:

Three ignorant mountain shepherds had said they saw a "vision," on May 13, 1917. They described it as a young woman, in brilliant light, who would not reveal her identity but said simply that she was "From Heaven." She asked the shepherd children to return to that spot on the same date of the month until October. Later she told them that she would reveal her identity and "Perform a public miracle so that everyone may believe."

Five thousand persons were present at the third "vision," when the children said that their messenger from Heaven had given them a secret and would perform the miracle in October.

About thirty thousand witnessed the fifth "vision," when again it was affirmed that on October 13th, on the spot, there would be *"A miracle, so that everyone may believe."*

On that now famous October 13th... a date which coincided with the power thrust of Communism in Russia... the "miracle" happened.

Over one hundred thousand persons were gathered on the mountain where the children had seen their "visions" and they experienced ten minutes of such terror that even today, over forty years later, a look of fear often comes to their eyes when they are asked to describe what they saw.

But their fear was replaced by a glorious hope... a hope which has begun to stir the hearts of millions behind the Iron Curtain where the message of Fatima is now penetrating.

Perhaps only those who have been afraid can really grasp the hope... can really bridge that chasm between wondering knowledge and active realization.

Anyone who *"realizes"* that this "miracle" happened (with a message from God to our age when whole nations might explode in mushroom clouds) *impatiently does something about it.*

That's why *we should meet the witnesses.*

If sometimes their testimony seems repetitious, we listen in awe to every word like a child learning a difficult lesson. Before such unbelievable reality... the most intelligent and best educated of us are like little children. *We are faced with a fact which has never before taken place in the history of man.*

To put it in a few simple words—the official words used by the Bishop of Fatima in his Pastoral Letter on the Miracle:

"Thousands upon thousands of persons... saw all the manifestations of the sun... a phenomenon which no astronomical observatory registered and thus was not natural... persons of every category and social class, believers and unbelievers, journalists of the principal Portuguese newspapers, and even persons some miles away..."

The incident is so unreal that only a parade of living witnesses can help us to realize

1. This is the first time in the history of man that God will have performed a miracle (excluding the Resurrection) at a predicted time and place to prove something;

2. It claims that War is caused by sin; Error will continue to

The three children to whom Our Lady appeared: (*left to right*) Jacinta and Francisco Marto and Lucia dos Santos.

spread from an atheistic Russia throughout the entire world, fomenting further war; several nations will be annihilated; *unless men stop offending God.* But each good person, by doing special things, can obtain mercy so that Russia (this is understood to mean the atheistic communists) will be converted and *there will be peace.* *The world has received an ultimatum.*

Would it not be sad indeed if religious prejudice, or the sheer weight of secularism, were to prevent the world from realizing this staggering fact?

Mr. Dominic Reis, of Holyoke, Massachusetts, was in

Dominic Reis (*left*) being interviewed on television by the author. Conversation in this chapter is verbatim transcription of the television interview.

Portugal in 1917.

"Did you hear that a miracle was predicted to take place at Fatima?" we asked him in early 1960.

"My father heard about it first. It was in the papers all over the country."

"How far from Fatima did you live, Dominic?"

"I lived at that time near Porto, over one hundred miles away."

"Were there very many people interested?"

"Yes. Suppose I explain from the beginning. I was 17 in May when it all began. Then in October, on the 11th, 1917, my father said to my mother, 'We're going up to Fatima. We're going to see what happens.'"

"Had it been announced, Dominic, that there would be a miracle on October 13th so that everyone would believe?"

"That's right. Lots of people thought it a lie. Lots of people was like... might as well say it... just like the government. The government didn't believe it either."

"But lots of people, like my mother and father, were all sensible in religion. And my father said, 'We're going up.' And he decided for my mother and myself just one day before, on the 11th. On the 12th we left at nine o'clock."

"Were there many people from your area who went to Fatima?"

"Yes. The train was full."

"How did you feel about all this as a young man of 17? Did you think your parents were right?"

"I felt... I felt something was going to happen."

"Was the prediction of this miracle announced in Church?"

"The Church said nothing at all... They were against it. If any Priest say anything about Fatima, even maybe something happen to him. Some churches in the area of Fatima were marred, stones thrown, anything to break down the coming of the people."

(Note: The government in Portugal at this time was similar to the Communist government which took over in Russia that same year.)

"Pardon repetition of this, Dominic, but it appears that one of the great facts of this day is that thousands of people, against almost insuperable obstacles, traveled on foot up this great mountain... over stones, opposed by soldiers, and in a cold rain. You had traveled with your family all the previous night and now, about what time did you come to where the miracle was predicted to happen?"

"We left Leiria at six o'clock in the morning. Was then only light rain."

"Were there many people?"

"Oh, yes! The little fields, the rocks, and everywhere you look... you see people! Some with little things on their heads.[1] We were all climbing that mountain just like nothing at all. Even I see people who did not expect to see anything, saying nothing will happen. And other people going all the way from Leiria without saying a word. I meet several people walking in silence, and some people..."

"When did you finally get to the Cova?"[2]

"We get there around noon time. Between half past eleven to around noon time. When we finally get there, there were soldiers...

"Everywhere we saw animals, trees, bushes. Very rough. And this National Guard, what we would call "weekend soldiers"... tried to stop us from going down into the Cova."

(Note: As we meet eyewitnesses of the miracle, it is well to bear in mind that our purpose is not primarily to prove that the miracle happened, but rather to reach a realization that it happened. The proof is incidental. We know of no one who denies the fact of the miracle... but we know of few who realize the fact. That is why we permit ourselves some leading questions with the witnesses, deliberately emphasizing again and again the salient features of this most extraordinary event).

"The crowd was too great for the soldiers to hold?"

"The crowd was breaking in one corner. When the soldiers move to protect that corner, another corner is breaking out.

---

1. Portuguese often carry baskets on their heads and since so many of these people had come from a distance, there were many carrying water and food.
2. This is the spot, near Fatima, where three children had predicted that a miracle would happen on that October day. Today it is a great paved amphitheater, but in 1917 it was just a great hollow, as though created by a meteor in some prehistoric age.

First thing you know, everybody got through."

"Did the soldiers finally give up?"

"What happened, happened because they couldn't control crowds... I was slightly wounded by one of the bayonets."[3]

"So finally you got down into the Cova with the crowd, and where did you go?"

"We got close to the tree where the children were. The three children we had heard about were there already..."

"The vision was reported to have appeared to these three children at that spot?"

"That's right. On the side was a big tree, and little small trees around, and the children were there. And now it was raining harder. There was a good three inches of water where I stood, and mud on the ground."

"Three inches of water on the ground?"

"Yes, three inches of water on the ground. I was soaking wet. I was... and then round noon time, the sun started breaking... we can see the sun..."

(Mr. Reis was now leaning forward in his chair, deeply moved by the vivid memory.)

"Now it was raining just like you open a faucet at your house. Rain! And then suddenly the rain stopped. The sun started to roll from one place to another place,

Dominic Reis

---

3. At this point Mr. Reis showed a scar on his hand from a wound inflicted by the bayonet of one of the soldiers as he, with many others, braved the pointed bayonets in pushing through to get to the Cova. Almost all the witnesses appearing in the pages of this book were interviewed in 1960, forty-three years after the miracle. Each of them recalls what happened "as though it were yesterday." We have used extensive photographs with the story of Mr. Reis to show his face and eyes as he recalled what happened. However, unfortunately, the photographs fall far short of the reality.

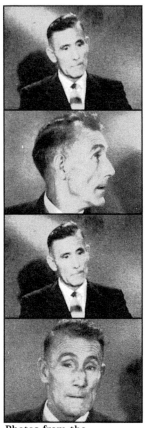

and changed blue, yellow, all colors! Then we see the sun come toward the children, toward the tree. Everybody was hollering out. Some start to confess their sins, 'cause there were no Priests around there.'"

"And the people started to confess their sins aloud, before everyone?"

"That's right. Even my mother grabbed me to her and started to cry, saying, 'It is the end of the world!' And we see the sun come right into the trees. And then the little children get up and turn around to the people and told the people, 'Pray and pray hard because everything is going to be all right.' And then the children walk to the tree, and talk in the direction of the tree, and we see the children bend down just like bow to somebody, I don't see what, but something was there because we see the children bend down, then

Photos from the television interview.

we see the children move the lips to talk to someone."

"Did you look at the sun without difficulty?"

"Yes, I could look at the sun without pain in the eyes. Everyone around me was making a tremendous noise. Because of all the noise, I was looking at the crowd as the sun was actually falling. Afterwards, I was told that it had turned upon itself and fallen down. But at that moment I saw it on my shoulder."

"What did you think of all this?"

"The people around me were saying they thought this was

the end of the world. They were very much afraid. Many seemed to think, and were saying, that the revolutionaries were going to throw bombs on the people, as did happen later when there was bombings by the people running the government at that time. Many were standing, but many others were on their knees and were crying and calling on the Blessed Virgin."

"How far away were you, Dominic, from where the children were?"

"I was, I'd say, between seventy-five and one hundred feet from the children and the tree."

"Did you get a chance to get close to the children?"

"Yes, when everything was finished. And the sun rolled back again the way it came in ..."

"What did the people do when they saw it roll back into the sky? Did they stop crying out?"

"The people knelt down and prayed real hard. And then Lucia (the eldest of the children) said to pray hard."

"Lucia said that God was too much offended?"

"That God was too much offended."

"Here are some photographs, Mr. Reis. Is this the way you remember it?"

"That's in my time. That's the way it was there."

"This next photograph, Dominic, was taken just a few minutes

Fatima: Noon,
October 13, 1917.

after the other. Everyone had begun to shout... they put their umbrellas down."

"We put the umbrellas down... Lucia start to talk to the people, one here, one bunch there, and some started to kiss the little kid, and then the wind started to blow real hard..."

"Dominic, we have talked to many witnesses who were there. All speak of 'the sun,' but could it have been the sun... or just so much like the sun that they thought it was the sun?"

"Well, for my part, it was the sun. But whether just a light or

The Miracle itself could not be photographed because of its brilliance.

Even for an eclipse of the sun, photographers use special equipment and "set up" in advance. Yet this was a phenomenon more brilliant than an eclipse. Photographs of the crowd seem as though taken at high noon. The light was visible thirty miles away, and appeared as a great red flash sixteen miles down in Leiria (were the angle of the view was such that the climax of the Miracle, the "falling", was not seen.)

The colors have been characterized as "monochromatic sectors" which appeared to revolve and to subsist without any known supports. In other words, the colors were not prismatic, but individual rays of brilliant color.

At least one book has already been written about the physical nature of the phenomenon in itself: Sciatizzi's *Fatima in the Light of Faith and Science.*

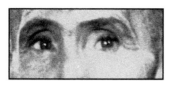

not, *there was something there.* I know for sure. The way the trees were coming down, the way the... I don't believe that the children would go to a tree and start moving lips to a tree. Must have been something there to talk to."

"You described this great fire, or light, or 'sun' as rolling out of the sky. You said that people thought it was the end of the world."

"It was a real sun like you see in the sky..."

"What about the colors...?"

"There were colors all around the sun. The sun rolled... and it was like the real sun... but the clouds didn't go with the sun. There were blue and different colors..."

"Did you think the world was going to be destroyed by *fire*?"

"Yes. Because... I can tell you one thing. My mother when she squeeze me, and say it's the end of the world, I see like the sun almost on top of my shoulder."

"Did all the people think they were going to be crushed by the sun?"

"That's right."

"But then, this matter of the rain and water to which so many testify. What happened with the water?"

"As soon as the sun went back in the right place the wind started to blow real hard, but the trees didn't move at all. The wind was blow, blow and in few minutes the ground was as dry as this floor here.[4] Even our clothes had dried. We were walking here and there, and our clothes... we don't feel at all. The clothes were dry and looked as though they had just come from the laundry. I believed. I thought: *Either I'm out of my mind or this was a miracle, a real miracle.*"

"Of course, Dominic, you were only one of thousands of

---

4. At this moment, Mr. Reis dramatically beat his foot against the wooden floor of the room where this interview took place.

witnesses. Newsmen were there who experienced it. And two days later the newspaper, *O Século*, told how the sun danced. Atheists were converted, and soon the Soviets (this is the term used for them in Portugal at this time) went out of power. But in the 1960's do you think the world is listening to this message?"

"I believe some, yes. I believe little by little some listen. But still quite a few all over the world don't listen to it."

Photograph of part of the crowd taken during the Miracle.

Close-ups of the crowd.

Chapter 2
THE ATHEISTS

A clique which denied the very existence of God... and held that religion was a stumbling block to social progress... had come to power in Portugal seven years before the miracle.

Its symbols were the triangle and the red star. Its "gospel" was from the pages of free thought and Marxism. It vowed to wipe out religion within two generations. It confiscated the property of all religious orders and drove them from the country. It banished the Cardinal Primate. It murdered the Royal Family down to the last child, and said that religion was the opiate of the people.

One of the principal Portuguese newspapers of this time was *O Século* ("The Century"), published in Lisbon. Through this newspaper (as well as through all channels of communication in Portugal) the government had discouraged all travel to Fatima with suggestions of violence and danger. Soldiers, armed with pointed bayonets, were placed around the top of the mountain to prevent crowds from assembling, as we remember from Mr. Reis' testimony.

Moreover, the government bullies had tried to "persuade" the children to retract their prophecy. But during forty-eight hours of imprisonment, the children withstood all threats and cajoleries.

Word of this spread through the country, and even beyond the borders of Portugal.

This, coupled with the strange events reported to have been seen on the mountain, largely explains why such a tremendous crowd braved a cold rain to climb—with donkeys, cars and carts, but the vast majority on foot—up the heights of that bleak mountain ninety miles beyond Lisbon on October 13, 1917.

On this same October 13th, another revolution was reaching its climax on the other side of Europe.

That revolution, too, had as its symbol a red star. And its slogans were the same as those which had echoed here in Portugal just seven years before: "Long live liberty! Down with religion! Long live democracy!"

Even more significant, the proponents of this atheistic revolution now breaking out on the other side of the world, like cancer in the weakened man, proclaimed it a *world revolution*. The red star was predicted to rise over all mankind before peace would come. The militant

The first page of the "funnies" in *O Século* presented the apparition of Fatima as death through starvation, with the caption: "Hunger! This is the true apparition... palpable and real!"

atheists who carried the red star taught that religion was a device to keep the peasantry of the world in subjection. The "Red Star" leaders cried out that not until the masses of the world would be educated in the realization that man is only a super-animal, to be ruled by principles of general benefit to the common herd rather than with any respect to personal rights, would the peasants be freed from the chains of poverty.

Much in the doctrine of this "Red Star" revolution held appeal to the masses of the world. It had as its slogan: "You have nothing to lose but your chains." It made poverty the world's only sin. It offered common distribution of wealth as the key to world peace and happiness.

The children claimed that their Visitor from Heaven spoke

of sins more awful than poverty. They said that shining from the hem of her robe was a great star—not a red star, but a star of light. And she spoke of what was going to happen in Russia and of wars which would come.

And she was going to perform a public miracle *"so that all may believe."*

What was the effect of the Miracle on the *unbelievers*?

There are at least seven scientifically objective facts:

1. *The time and place* of this event were *predicted in advance;*
2. *A light* of extraordinary power was seen over a radius of more than twenty miles like a *"Catherine wheel" of fireworks*, sending off great shafts of colored light which tinted objects on the ground;
3. It plummeted toward the earth after several minutes, assuming such a gigantic nearness that the tens of thousands of witnesses *thought it was the end of the world;*
4. The great ball of fire stopped *just as it was about to crash upon the earth,* and returned into the sky;
5. It came from and went back to the location of *the sun*, so that those who saw it actually thought it was the sun;
6. The top of the mountain where this occurred, which had been drenched by several hours of constant rain, *suddenly dried* within a matter of minutes;
7. *Tens of thousands of witnesses* of all classes and of various creeds, extended over an area of about six hundred square miles.

Colonel Frederico Oom, professor of the Faculty of Sciences and Director of the Lisbon Observatory, stated:

"If it were a cosmic phenomenon, astronomical and meteorological observatories would not have failed to record it. And this is precisely what is missing: that inevitable recording of all the disturbances in the world system, no matter how small they may be..."

Asked if this phenomenon was of a psychological nature the scientist replied that it might have been, but as an astronomer he could definitely affirm one thing:

"It is completely foreign to the branch of science that I cultivate."

This statement by Colonel Oom was published in *O Século* in Lisbon shortly after the Miracle occurred, with the intention of giving the only possible explanation which science could offer: collective suggestion.

However, as the evidence has been studied and evaluated, it becomes absolutely certain that the phenomenon was not the

Front page of *O Século* reprints the Miracle.

result of mass hypnosis or collective suggestion.

The reasons are:

1. It was witnessed over a large area by persons not in the crowd;

2. Among the crowd were scientists and "unbelievers" who viewed the phenomenon not only with objectivity, but with particular care to protect themselves from the possibility of collective suggestion.

For example, we have the Baron of Alvaiazere, who carefully took all precautions outlined by Gustave le Bon in his *Psychology of the Crowd*. The Baron had not expected a miracle and wanted to be sure that he would not be the victim of suggestion. He died in 1955, and in a deposition to the Canonical Committee he stated: "...An indescribable impression overtook me I only know that I cried out: 'I believe! I believe! I believe!' And tears ran from my eyes. I was amazed, in ecstasy before the demonstration of Divine Power... converted in that moment."

Doctor Garrett, a professor from the University of Coimbra, in detailed testimony describes that he feared some impairment to his retina, covered his eyes and turned in an opposite direction, opened his eyes again... and continued to see the miracle.

Several other men of science who were actual witnesses, testified to the objective reality of the phenomenon and added that no natural explanation could be given.

Pio Sciatizzi, S.J., scientist who published a critique of the Miracle in Rome, says: "Of the historic reality of this event there can be no doubt whatsoever. That it was outside and against known laws can be proved by certain simple scientific considerations." And he concludes:

"Given the indubitable reference to God, and the general context of the event, it seems that we must attribute to Him alone *the most obvious and colossal miracle of history...*"

Perhaps as amazing as the "miracle" itself is the revelation which the children claimed that Heaven was asserting:

World War I (then at its peak) would soon end, but another...
a more terrible war... would begin soon unless people recog-
nized that war is a punishment for sin. Men had to cease
offending God, Who was too grievously offended by too many.

Moreover, following this "More terrible war"...which would
come even "Within the reign of the next Pope"...an atheistic
*power would arise in Russia and extend its errors "**through-***
out the entire world**," **fomenting further war**, and "**several
***entire nations will be annihilated**."*

But again, what effect did the miracle of Fatima have...
objectively, historically... on the nonbelievers who ruled
Portugal at that time?

Chapter 3
EFFECT ON PORTUGAL

Many tensions in Portugal prepared the climate for the revolution which took place in 1910, almost identical to those in Russia in 1917. During our recent research in Portugal on the Miracle of the Sun, we came to know a young man whose father was part of that revolution. He is a living witness to the nature of the revolution and to much of the mystery of which this book speaks.

He is self-confident, energetic, uninhibited. He speaks freely of political concentration camps conducted by the present regime in Portugal, and of a new revolution which he predicts will "certainly come."

But without any fear of those concentration camps, he showed us some literature from the early days of the 1910 revolution. It reads almost exactly like the pamphlets used by communists all over the world today. The cover of the major pamphlet is distinguished by a symbol that is now all too familiar—*a red star*.

And while this man (whose identity we shall withhold) is financially successful, entertains in a pleasant home and drives about in a pleasant car, he is fearlessly indignant about the exploitation of labor in Portugal. He has never bothered to go through the ceremony of marriage with the lovely woman who shares his life. They have no children. He is a "freethinker" who mingles a disarming charm and enthusiasm for the working classes with a disdain of religion and of Portugal's present government.

This, partially, is the *face of communism*. It is often a pleasant face. This man is one whom everyone might like instinctively. He is outgoing; he is filled with a zest for life; and his concern for the social inequity in his country seems sincere, even though—by his own intelligence, warm personality and qualities of leadership—he himself has risen somewhat above those supposed inequities.

Those who liken communism to religion—even though communism is the antithesis of true religion—make a good analogy. That is why communism is the most insidious evil in history. It is the absolute heresy, which explodes from a mere denial of the existence of God into a gospel of superanimalism.

And now that we are about to speak of the effect of the Miracle of the Sun on Portugal, the first distinction we must make is between the nation and individuals within the nation.[1]

The first is history, and the second touches upon the mystery of man and of his free will.

Lenin had said to Trotsky in Paris, in those early days of plotting Marxism for the world:[2]

"Our revolution is international. We will begin simultaneously on the Iberian Peninsula (Portugal and Spain) and in Russia, and one day we will close the revolution across Europe." The year chosen for simultaneous revolt in both East and West was 1910.

The deep connections between Marxism and the free thinkers of the French revolution was most apparent in the mixed forces which swept the revolution to success in Portugal right on schedule in 1910. But only in Portugal.

That same year, Germany declared war on Russia, and Lenin declared:

"It is expedient that we wait until the Czarist armies are weakened in the conflict with the Kaiser."

So the Russian revolt waited until 1917, the year of the

---

1. *Fatima in the Light of History*, by Costa Brochado, translated and edited by George Boehrer of Marquette University, published by Bruce, 1955, is literally what the title suggests: A narration of facts of Fatima as history. It presents the Miracle of the Sun in the light of the entire history of Portugal, with a background of the early framework of the nation up to and including the 1910 revolution.
2. *Russia Will Be Converted*, by John M. Haffert, published by A.M.I., 1950, Chapters I and II.

Miracle of the Sun—the year that the revolution was already seven years in power in Portugal.

The backbone of the Red Star revolution in Portugal was a secret organization known as "Carbonaria." Magalhaes Lima and Afonso Costa (two names to keep in mind) were the extremists in this movement. Each held high office in the Republic. But the nominal founder of the party was an engineer named Antonio Maria da Silva.

The Miracle of the Sun never appeared more truly an "explosion of the Supernatural" than to these Red Star rulers of Portugal. They had identified their revolution with atheism. They taught that religion was the opiate of the people. And they suddenly were faced with a miracle witnessed by one-seventieth of the total population of the nation!

Antonio Maria da Silva was one of the first to bow before the awesomeness of the Miracle. He began to speak shortly after that eventful October 13, 1917, of conciliation with the Church. But at once his life was threatened; he was covered with insults and defamations; and there followed a period of terrorism in Portugal such as few areas of the world have ever known.

So recent a period in history is difficult to evaluate. There are so many facts available that their relative importance often becomes obscure. But one salient fact is clear:

It was the Miracle of the Sun which defeated the Red Star in Portugal.

The defeat was not overnight. It took several years, and is not yet resolved. Briefly, here are some notable facts: immediately after the Miracle, the atheistic government—which like most governments in early years was built on coalition—tried to purge those elements which might "give in" to the Miracle. Meanwhile it sought to discountenance the Miracle and ridicule those who believed it even though faced with a mass of witnesses scattered in every corner of the land.

Nine days after the Miracle of the Sun a car came from Santarem to Fatima. An oak tree, which was supposed to be that upon which the apparitions appeared, was hacked down. Some religious articles which had been erected at the spot by some devout persons were confiscated.

The following day, three newspapers in Portugal carried front page headlines about the "ridiculous" emblems of super-stition now brought to Santarem.

The simple little tree (which actually was not the proper tree at all, but one which had grown close by) and the few religious articles were displayed on Sa da Bandeira Square in Santarem. And in *O Século*, the same newspaper which gave us the "offi-cial" description of the Miracle of the Sun, on October twen-ty-fourth we read the following: "Today the pilgrimage of vis-itors continued here to the trunk of the apparition tree of the Virgin of Fatima and to the objects which credulity had placed there, and which yesterday arrived in Santarem.

"...Last night many people organized a parade in the form of a procession, led by drums. In it were carried the branches of the famous apparition tree of the Virgin of Fatima, the myrtle arch, the burning lanterns, the cross, and other objects which the faithful had placed on the improvised altar.

"The marchers chanted picturesque 'litanies' and in measured steps went through the principal streets of the city. The proces-sion broke up in Sa de Bandeira Square where it had begun."

The "litanies" referred to in the paper were sacrilegious. And although many persons of the country were afraid of the regime, the religious soul of Portugal—awakened by tens of thousands of witnesses of the Miracle of the Sun—was pro-foundly shocked. On October twenty-seventh at least one newspaper had the courage to express much of what was in the hearts of many Portuguese:

"So much baseness exists in Portugal... the country can

descend no further on the road to shame and vileness."
However, the remark of this newspaper, just two weeks after
the Miracle of the Sun, was unfortunately exaggerated. There
was much greater shame to come.

Arturo dos Santos, the Administrator of Fatima, was becoming ever more embittered by the defeat which he felt. He had
been only the administrator of a small area, but certainly he
had had hopes of rising in the new government. Now, from
what had happened in his relatively unimportant area, the
whole revolution was jeopardized.

In December a special "propaganda mission" was sent from
Lisbon. The humiliated Santos received it in Ourem. The mission proceeded up to Fatima where speeches were delivered
against the existence of God, at the spot of the apparitions.
Next day newspapers read:

"Warm acclamations... were raised to the Republic (on the
mountain at Fatima)... from afar off poor fanatical women sang
the Divine praises. This proves the necessity of repeating missions such as this. The following telegram was sent to the
President of the Republic from Fatima: 'The free thinkers of
Ourem... salute the Republic in the person of its first magistrate
and hope to see liberty of the national conscience guaranteed.'"

However, where propaganda missions had worked wonders
in the past (backed as they were with force), there now seemed
to have been a greater "propaganda mission" from Heaven. As
it turned out, the atheistic revolution was doomed.

Dissension spread and popular resistance grew. Soon the
revolutionaries permitted a conservative from their midst,
named Sidonio Pais, to assume the Presidency. But Pais
became more and more liberal to religion, and only one year
after he had come to power, he was riddled with bullets as he
was leaving for the Rossio station in Lisbon. He died on a table
at Saint Joseph's hospital, with a crucifix over his breast.

The period which followed is described as one of "absolute terrorism." Bombings took place daily throughout the entire country. Brochado summarizes it thus:

"The extremist press treated ministers of state as criminals, and civic groups intimidated the deputies while authorities terrorized and shot them."

Meanwhile, the Church seemed to have abandoned the subject of Fatima. Of the three children, only Lucia was alive. Francisco had died in April, 1919, and Jacinta died on February 20, 1920.

But crowds continued to go to Fatima in ever increasing numbers. The impact of the Miracle of the Sun was growing as more and more witnesses told their neighbors of what they had seen, and these in turn told others. In 1920, so great were the crowds going to Fatima that strong detachments of the Republican Guard and of the army were posted there to intimidate the people. But the crowd was not frightened despite sword thrusts and violence. Arturo dos Santos, still Administrator of Ourem, was gaining favor with his superiors by violence against crowds going to Fatima. On May 15th he received a warm letter of congratulations from Lisbon, to show "profound sympathy for the manner in which you acted on the question of the pretended miracle at Fatima, by which Jesuitical and clerical reaction attempts to exploit the ignorance of the people."

In 1922, with crowds at Fatima still increasing, agents blew up a little chapel which had been built at the spot of the apparitions. During this same week bombs went off almost everywhere in Portugal, especially in Lisbon, Porto, and Viana do Castelo.

Two months later the largest crowd to gather at Fatima since the Miracle, came in reparation. The Bishop, a few weeks later, appointed a commission to look into the Miracle.

That year (1922) probably was the turning point. The revolution had spent five years of fury and force, but the stoic and

Fatima, March 13, 1922

deep faith of the people—which this revolution had vowed to wipe out in two generations—was coming forth with a strength which the revolutionaries would never have dreamed possible. By 1923 single crowds at Fatima had reached the number of seventy thousand, and by 1926, according to newspapers at the time, the amazing number of four hundred thousand people gathered at the Cova and the highway was lined with automobiles for miles.

By 1927 the revolutionaries had exhausted themselves in internecine struggle and assassinations and were bankrupt. A conservative coalition persuaded a quiet professor from the University of Coimbra, a man known to be of deep religious faith and an expert on government and economy, to help salvage the ruins of the nation. His name was Doctor Oliveira Salazar.

From that day Portugal changed. Many problems remained to be solved—even as there are problems in every country, whether economic or racial or political.

But the change could be described as hardly less than "wonderful." Cardinal Cerejeira, Primate of Portugal, told us that he considered this change in Portugal to be the second "miracle" of Fatima.

And what happened to the great revolutionaries?

Lima died in disillusion. Although he was one of the two men who had guaranteed that religion would be extinct in Portugal within two generations, his memoirs read much like the final testament of Lenin:

"What goes on about me makes me uneasy. Politics, always an apostolate for me, has become a business... In the time of the most base interests in which we live, everyone wants to govern... no one is trusted..."

As for Costa: He fled to Paris, abandoning the revolution and his country forever. And, oddly enough, this man who had denied the existence of God and vowed to wipe out religion, fell into spiritualism. He ended by being tortured with an obsession of the supernatural.

Since too many pages would be needed to describe the fate of all the great revolutionaries, we would like to close this chapter by a personal experience in Lisbon.

Lisbon had been proclaimed in 1915 to be the atheist capital of the world. The revolutionaries had considered it to be the *most atheistic city on earth.*[3]

Just thirty-four years after the Miracle of the Sun, a "peace congress" was held in Lisbon in conjunction with the closing of the Holy Year for all the world outside of Rome at Fatima.

The great government buildings of Lisbon, which had housed and seen so many of the horrors of the revolution, were now opened to discussion of world peace based on the message of Fatima! Speakers at this congress were from all corners of the world.

The Archbishop of Mitilene presided. The first rows were filled with some thirty Bishops. Delegates were present from

---

3. *Fatima in the Light of History,* page 230.

the Portuguese government and from every corner of the world. Bishop Sheen from the United States was guest chairman, and among the speakers were Canon Barthas (one of the early "International" apostles of Fatima from France) and the great ex-communist from England, Douglas Hyde.

Most of the speeches—on peace in the face of communist aggression—were quite long. But after serving eight difficult years in propagation of the message of Fatima, sensing world fear of an atomic war, it took this writer only a few minutes to say what was in his heart:

"What further proof does one need of the nearness of God... of the solution of the East-West crisis, ...than this meeting, in this very city of Lisbon, in these very buildings where thirty-four years ago were enacted laws to abolish all religion from this nation?

"Nunc dimittis servum tuum... because our eyes have already seen the sign of our salvation."

The writer does not know whether there were tears in many eyes because he had them in his own. But he remembers the emotional applause which rang through the hall long after he had finished.

The next day, thirty-fourth anniversary of the Miracle of the Sun, there were some *million* persons at Fatima for the ceremonies. Newsmen described the crowd as "one of the greatest aggregations of human beings in history".

Only *thirty-four years had passed*, in this former "world capital of atheism," since the Miracle of the Sun.

Chapter 4
THE MIRACLE LESSENED

Eight miles down the mountain from Fatima is the town of Ourem, mentioned several times in the previous chapter. It features importantly in the great facts of Fatima because it is the administrative center of the Fatima area.

There, two months before the actual occurrence of the Miracle of the Sun, occurred one of the most horrifying of inhumanities: A threat of death by boiling oil upon the three children who claimed that a miracle was to take place.

Because of this, the children announced something about the miracle which cannot be measured, cannot be even proved... except from their affirmation. This is fraught with the mystery of man's relation to his fellow man, and of all men to God. It is the *mystery of the part of the Miracle of the Sun which never happened.*

During two days of imprisonment, officials tried to get the children to admit that everything that they had told the crowd was either put up to them by someone else, or was a hoax of their own making.

Undoubtedly it was the behavior of the children under threat of death which did most to convince the nation that they had indeed been telling the truth and that something was going to happen at Fatima on October 13th. Even today, some who are concerned that the Miracle of the Sun might be exaggerated, find it easier to believe because of the heroism of the children in the Ourem prison.

When the children reached the jail, seven-year-old Jacinta began to cry. Her nine-year-old brother Francisco tried to quiet and console her. Ten-year-old Lucia said softly: "Why must you cry, Jacinta?"

"Because we are going to die without ever seeing our mothers and fathers again. None of them have come to see us. They

The parents of Jacinta (Mr. and Mrs. Marto) photographed at the exhumation of Jacinta's body in 1951.

don't care for us any more. I want to see my mother!"

For this small child of seven, forcible separation from her mother was perhaps greater torture than physical injury. The prospect of dying did not seem as terrible as did the awful loneliness. Whenever she had cried her mother soon made things right. But now...?

"Don't cry, Jacinta," Francisco said, "The Lady told us to make sacrifices for sinners, and we can offer this sacrifice for sinners."

At this Jacinta instantly choked back her sobs, raised her face and wiped the hot tears. Then, simultaneously motivated, all three children... entering the jail... looked Heavenward and repeated a prayer the beautiful Lady had taught them: "My Jesus, all this is for love of You and for sinners."

There were several men in the prison at the time. At sight of the three children with their frightened eyes and trembling lips, not one of the men failed to show sympathy. One of the men told them not to be afraid because seeing a vision, or even telling a lie, was not enough to merit death. The children were on the verge of tears. Deeply touched by the children's obvious terror, all the inmates of the jail began a chorus of reassurances...

laughing the matter off and trying to get the children to laugh.
But it was to no avail.

"Why don't you tell the secret?" one of the men urged.
"Why should you care?" Another took up, "Yes, tell him the
old secret. There can't be any harm in that. Why should you
care if he knows the secret?"

It was Jacinta, the most outwardly distressed of the three,
who answered with broken voice:

"Never. We would never tell because the Lady would not
want it. We would rather die."

The men were impressed.

At the end of two hours Jacinta was taken from the jail first,
ostensibly to be burned alive in a vat of boiling oil. "The oil is
boiling," she was told back in the courtroom just across the
court from the jail. "If you tell the secret we shall let you go,
otherwise...

Jacinta, no longer crying, remained silent.

"Take her away!" growled the judge. "Throw her in the oil!"
And a guard grabbed the child by the arm and wheeled her
from the room.

While this was going on, Francisco whispered to Lucia, as
though to reassure them both: "If they kill us we shall soon be
in Heaven. Nothing else counts. I hope Jacinta wouldn't be
frightened. I should say a Hail Mary for her." And he took off
his cap to pray.

"What are you saying?" a puzzled guard inquired.

Naively, Francisco replied: "I am saying a Hail Mary for
Jacinta to give her courage."

A moment later he himself was dragged by the arm before
the judge.

"All right now," the judge glowered, not at all pleased by his
failure with the seven-year-old Jacinta. "Your sister has
already been boiled in oil because she didn't tell the secret.

Now it's your turn. Out with it! If you want to save yourself and the other girl, tell it."

"I can't," Francisco protested, "I can't tell it to anyone!"

"Take him away!" shouted the magistrate. "Throw him in, too!" And as the guard began to drag Francisco toward the door through which Jacinta had disappeared, the judge and all about him waited anxiously hoping and expecting to see the little lad break down. But tight lipped, with the same expression which must have lighted the faces of the first martyrs, Francisco went without even turning about.

Probably Arturo dos Santos in his anger would have been very happy to really boil the children in oil, but he had merely removed them to a locked room.

Now frustrated, but not anxious for a bloody clash with thousands of indignant citizens at such an early stage of this strange conflict with an "apparition," the civil authorities decided to send the children back to their home.

It was August 15th, a great religious Feast Day, and the children were set free.

The powerful anti-religious government which had reigned in Portugal for seven years had failed... with all its pomp and power and awesomeness... before the simple faith of three illiterate peasant children. Apparently cut off by the Church and deprived of the consolation of even seeing their parents before going to what they certainly believed to be a horrible death, the children remained faithful to their account of the vision.

Had the children been telling the truth? Even hardened members of the revolutionary government could not help but wonder. Strong men had broken down under an ordeal such as these children had endured. Yet they had never once contradicted their extraordinary story.

When the present writer spoke of this incident with the eldest of the children, her eyes were shy and doelike, without a trace of resentment, and without even a trace of satisfaction

Today the spot of the apparition in the field of Valinhos is marked by this single monument constructed by the Hungarians in exile after the Hungarian revolt against Communism in 1956.

with herself at having passed through such an ordeal. And when we asked if she had really expected to die that day in Ourem prison, she answered with a quiet dignity, as though affirming no more important a fact than whether or not it was a rainy or sunny day:

"I thought Francisco and Jacinta had already been killed."

And now we come to the "mystery."

The vision appeared to the children on August nineteenth on the mountain of Fatima in a field some distance from where the apparitions normally took place. It was four days after the imprisonment, and the children explained to the Lady that they had not been able to keep their "date" with her on August 13th because they had been imprisoned. They reported that the apparition, by a sad nod of the head, acknowledged that she knew this, and then said:

"Because of this the miracle promised for October will not be as great."

What could be served by the announcement—now so close to the predicted time of the miracle—that it would be "not as great" as intended? Who would ever be able to know how great the miracle would have been? Might it have been seen over a greater area? Perhaps as far as Lisbon? Might it have been of greater duration? Might there have been other phenomena in addition to those witnessed like the whirling light in the sky, the appearance that the world was coming to an end, and the concluding tangibility of a sudden drying out of a water-soaked mass of people standing in what had been slushy pools?

Perhaps we shall never know. And that is one of the mysteries—not so much about what might have been, but a mystery of what is: That the actions of a few evil men can affect all of us.

Chapter 5
THE WITNESS WHO COULD NOT BELIEVE

Administrator of Ourem, Arturo dos Santos, refused to bow to the miracle.

He not only fought a war against the children "even unto death," threatening to burn them alive in boiling oil, but he fought a war against the crowds with squadrons of soldiers armed with swords and bayonets. Indeed, he fought a daily, haunting struggle, hour by hour, against the mysterious "Lady" of the Fatima mountain.

And this leads to a point of very great importance:

"If God wanted to change Russia," someone might ask, "then why does He not perform a Miracle of the Sun over Moscow?"

Arturo dos Santos helps us to understand; *miracles in themselves do not cause conversion.*

If some men do not accept God when they look into the immensity of the universe, or into the microscopic intricacy of the atom, then how can we expect them to acknowledge His existence over other phenomena, which—no matter how marvelous or unexpected—could never hope to exceed these wonders to which we are daily witnesses?

Furthermore, to see a miracle, and *to realize what one is seeing,* are two different things.

First there is a feeling of complete *unreality*—as though one has been dreaming, as though one were suffering hallucinations. What is witnessed is so unreal against the background of life's experience that the mind at first rejects it as not being real at all.

The present writer's experience of having witnessed a dramatic cure at Fatima emphasizes this fact. It was the cure of a

This picture was taken by a cameraman from Lisboa Films at the very moment I was running down the steps. The cured girl seems unable to realize her good fortune.

twenty-one year-old girl named Arminda Campos, ill for thirteen years and dying of a complication of three diseases. She had been in seven hospitals and undergone nine major operations before being brought to Fatima. She had not come there in the hope of a cure, but because she knew she was dying and wanted to visit there before her death. During all her thirteen years of illness, in imitation of one of the children of Fatima she had offered her sufferings "for the conversion of sinners and in reparation for the sins of the world."

Standing in front of her pallet one could not have the slightest inkling that this pitiable, dying person was about to be the center of an "explosion of the supernatural" just as marvelous as the one about which this book is written.

She was *instantly cured.*

We actually walked around her as she was getting up, and saw the blankets shrink upon her body. The great tumor had disappeared instantly. Within two hours we saw dry, clear scars on the girl's side where just before there had been two great, running incisions made by a surgeon's scalpel.

We will not go into the details of the cure here.[1] Our purpose is to analyze the effect of this curative miracle on those

---

1. For details see *Russia Will Be Converted.*

who saw it as a prelude to understanding the effect of the Miracle of the Sun on the witnesses who will soon appear in these pages.

First there was the writer's own experience of *NO emotional reaction.*

Even seeing the girl staring with almost ecstatic expression as she moved her hand in awe at the places in her side where scars had appeared, the writer felt no more emotion than might have been experienced under any happy circumstance.

It was fully *two hours* before the tremendous event which had just happened crossed the chasm from understanding to realization and evoked the marveling exclamation: "I have seen the Hand of God!"

Although one might consider it necessary to believe what his own eyes had seen, *because it was so completely contradictory to normal reality* and experience the mind and emotions had instinctively rejected it as *unreal.*

More remarkable than the writer's reaction to the cure of Arminda Campos was that of her own father.

This good man had seen his daughter progress, through various stages of illness over a period of thirteen years, to the door of death. And now, in a moment, he saw her walking about perfectly normal, cured of an almost total paralysis, of a great tumor, of incisions in her side, and even of the debility which would necessarily follow from her long immobility.

Although the nurses were radiant with joy, this man made no move to speak to his daughter or to embrace her. Indeed he showed no emotion whatsoever for perhaps an hour after the cure.

Then suddenly he cried out across the hospital room in which his daughter had been segregated from the crowds, ran to her and embraced her, weeping *in the final realization that he was not dreaming.*

We are not asking any one to believe in this particular cure. We are testifying only as to reactions *personally experienced and witnessed*. And in the light of this experience, the Miracle of the Sun on October 13, 1917, was of extraordinary character not merely in itself, but *in its effect on the witnesses*.

The emotions of the crowd on that mountain on October 13, 1917, were literally shredded. Most of the crowd was stricken with terror. They believed it was the end of the world.

Then suddenly the terror was lifted. There followed a tremendous feeling of relief, of joy at having been spared burning destruction. And in addition to all this, when the phenomenon was over, there was a *second* miracle when suddenly the entire mountain top—before that moment a sea of water and mud—became dry. *And they could feel it with their hands.*

But for us who were not there, *does it not still seem unreal?*

We can understand why some elements of the miracle such as the fact of the mountain suddenly becoming dry are not discussed much by most writers. These "extra" elements were more personal, and heighten the feeling of unreality in those who were not there.

But it is very probable that many of the witnesses, after panic followed by sudden relief, would have thought the whole thing a dream if *each one* had not had a personal *tangible* evidence that they had been witnesses to an "explosion of the Supernatural."

The captain of the regiment of soldiers on the mountain that day—with orders to prevent the gathering of the crowd —was converted instantly. Apparently so were hundreds of other unbelievers, as their testimony will show.

Yet, here is Arturo dos Santos, the Administrator of Ourem, who had received more evidence than anyone, and who turned away and still claimed there was no God, and that the red star would continue to fight through the world against the Lady of the Star of Light.

And this poor man's lonely death in 1955 refusing the Sacraments, leaves us with one of the most sobering thoughts about man in the atomic age of Communism.[2]

2. Arturo dos Santos died June 27, 1955. He could not have a religious burial, but in December of that year an interesting article appeared in *Stella*, the outstanding religious magazine of Portugal, which revealed something not previously known. A pious woman approached Santos in June, 1920 (less than three years after the miracle) to ask permission to install a statue in the little Chapel at Fatima. After hesitating, suddenly *he gave permission*, stipulating that it be done when there were no crowds and that *she should not reveal that he had given permission*. (This was revealed by the woman in question to the Baron of Alvaiazere, who described it in a letter to the Viscount of Montelo on June 5, 1920.)

On April 7, 1942, when this same statue was being carried in triumphant procession from Fatima to Lisbon, Santos was in the crowd when it passed through Ourem, and he was heard to declare: "I am not at all in favor of religion and of priests... but when I saw the image of the Vision I felt inwardly something which I cannot explain...

Chapter 6
Distant Witnesses

The area in which the Miracle was visible was approximately six hundred square miles. Many witnesses who saw the phenomenon from a distance were non-believers who disdained the "credulous" who had gone to the mountain. Others were prevented from going because school or work claimed their presence... or relatives, who did not believe, restrained them.

Father Joaquim Lourenço

Anyone going to Fatima today can speak with Father Joaquim Lourenço, Canon lawyer of the Diocese of Leiria, who saw it from a distance of nine miles.

Father Lourenço was a school boy then, and was with his brother and some other children in the village of Alburitel. They thought it was the end of the world. Both Father Joaquim and his brother subsequently became priests. Father Lourenço tells us:

"I feel incapable of describing what I saw. I looked fixedly at the sun which seemed pale and did not hurt my eyes.

"Looking like a ball of snow, revolving on itself, it suddenly seemed to come down in a zigzag, menacing the earth. Terrified, I ran and hid myself among the people, who were weeping and expecting the end of the world at any moment. It was a crowd which had gathered outside our local village school and we had all left classes and run into the streets because of the cries and surprised shouts of men and women who were in the street in front of the school when the miracle began.

"There was an unbeliever there who had spent the morning mocking the 'simpletons' who had gone off to Fatima just to see an ordinary girl. He now seemed paralyzed, his eyes fixed on the sun. He began to tremble from head to foot, and lifting up his arms, fell on his knees in the mud, crying out to God.

"But meanwhile the people continued to cry out and to weep, asking God to pardon their sins. We all ran to the two chapels in the village, which were soon filled to overflowing. During those long moments of the solar prodigy, objects around us turned all colors of the rainbow... When the people realized that the danger was over, there was an explosion of joy."

At San Pedro de Muel, some thirty miles from Fatima, the Portuguese writer, Afonso Vieira was on the veranda of his house at noon. Suddenly he was gripped by astonishment. Over the mountain at Fatima he saw the solar phenomenon taking place!

He called to his wife and mother-in-law to come and see. Mr. Vieira's widow gave us her deposition in 1960, confirming it.

In the United States, in Somerville, New Jersey, we met Mr. Albano Barros, a successful building contractor who was a child in a village near Minde, about eight miles from Fatima. Though only twelve years old at the time, he remembers the

"Miracle of the Sun",
painted by Alan Sorrell.

miracle as though it had happened yesterday.

"I was watching sheep, as was my daily task, and suddenly there, in the direction of Fatima, I saw the sun fall from the sky. I thought it was the end of the world."

We asked if he remembers that it had been raining and whether afterward his clothes were dry.

"I was so distracted that I remember nothing but the falling sun. I cannot even remember whether I took the sheep home, whether I ran, or what I did."

Mrs. Guilhermina Lopes da Silva is now living at twenty Rua de Nossa Senhora da Encarnacao in Leiria, sixteen miles from the place where the miracle occurred.

Mrs. da Silva had seen the crowds passing through Leiria in great numbers. She wanted very much to join them going to Fatima to see whether the miracle predicted by the children would happen.

"But I could not go," she testifies today, "because my husband was an unbeliever. I was looking toward the mountain at noon when suddenly I saw a great red flash in the sky.

"I called two men who were working for us. They, of course, saw it, too.

"One of my relatives, Mr. Louis Lopes from Arrabalde de Santa Margarida, went to Fatima and told us afterward that although he had taken every precaution to avoid the rain (because he suffered from bronchitis) he was soaked through from his feet to his waist. But as the sun came down from the sky he noticed, to his astonishment, that he was completely dry.

"And my former neighbor, Dona Nazare Pinheiro, when she came back from Fatima that day, told me that when she had seen the sun coming down like a spinning wheel, she was so frightened that she fell to her knees reciting the Act of Contrition, believing it to be indeed the end of the world."

The phenomenon was not completely visible in Leiria... which was only sixteen miles away... perhaps because of the contour of the land.

Fatima is in the midst of the Serra Aire Mountains, and although the mountain is itself about three thousand feet high, even today one has actually to reach the very top of the mountain... within a range of one mile... to see the tower of the Basilica which is at least sixty-five feet above the average level of the Cova.

Yet on sea level a tower sixty-five feet high can be seen from a distance of fourteen miles, because only the curvature of the earth (given adequate illumination and clear atmosphere) limits the range of visibility. But at Fatima, both the angle of the mountain over which the phenomenon occurred, and the contour of surrounding mountains, limit visibility.

Just how high the phenomenon was above the mountain is impossible to determine. There was a factor on this day far more limiting than distance: It had been raining over the entire area.

Everything considered, the startling brilliance of the phenomenon, seen over such a great area, and with such fearful effect upon all who witnessed it, must have been something akin to the effect of an atomic explosion.[1]

---

1. Witnesses say that they could look upon the 'sun' "without harm to the eyes." They specifically mention that the light did not harm their eyes because they considered this one of the aspects of the miracle. While the phenomenon could not actually have been the sun, almost all witnesses said that for them it really was the sun which danced and then plummeted from the sky. Here the testimony of the photographs taken during the miracle provide truly valuable evidence: The brilliance in the sky was so great that the phenomenon itself could not be photographed, and photographs of the crowd show that they looked upon a light so brilliant that many shaded their eyes... and the photographs are so clear that they could have been taken only in *full* sunlight.

Chapter 7
UNIVERSALITY OF TESTIMONY

Even on the day before the Miracle a sizable crowd gathered, seeking preferred places. Speaking of this crowd (already large the day before the Miracle) Maria da Capelinha, from Moita, about a mile from the Cova, testifies:

"There were so many people that it was hard to believe. They made such a noise that I could hear them even as far away as my own village. They had to sleep out in the open, completely uncovered, because there was no shelter in the Cova."

The next day the crowd increased all through the morning.

Doctor José Garrett, a Professor from the Faculty of Sciences of the University of Coimbra, was standing on the rim of the Cova with a commanding view of the entire area. He was armed with powerful binoculars so that he could observe not only the crowd, but also the spot of the apparitions.

Amazed at the size of the crowd "which was scattered over a large field which stretched at my feet," he made a count by taking a total of persons in the area closest to him, and then dividing that area into the total area of the crowd. *By this method he counted a hundred thousand.*

His estimate is credible because he was a precise witness.

When we asked most persons, for example, about the time of the miracle, answers were invariably vague. But Doctor Garrett had noted almost every passing moment "according to the official standard by government decree that coordinated our time standard with that of the belligerent countries..." (This explains what to many may seem a mystery: Most witnesses placed the miracle near noon. But "by the clock" it was after one thirty, because "official" time in Portugal was advanced to coincide with the time on the battlefront in France. The time was *solar* noon.)

Maria Teresa of Chainca, who, as a fifty-nine year-old

housewife, gave us her deposition on February 6, 1960, was standing about a hundred feet from the place of the apparitions, and she said that even there "many people were pressed together."

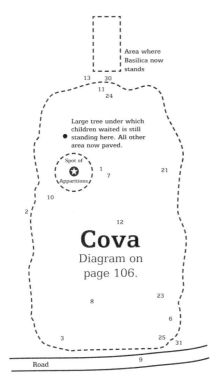

It is this kind of detailed evidence, using testimony from the entire area, which gives us a picture of the true size of the crowd. *Having studied the Cova and the testimony*, this writer is convinced that *the crowd was perhaps greater than the one hundred thousand* estimated by Doctor Garrett.

Our detailed interrogation of many witnesses also has clarified other points which before had been obscure, such as the universality of the testimony, sudden clarity of the atmosphere, the wind which moved across the mountain without touching the trees and suddenly dried everyone and everything. Many of these phenomena, which even to the present writer for many years sounded vaguely like nothing but "stories" or side effects which people might have imagined, have emerged with startling clarity.

Maria Teresa adds her testimony to all the others, and like all others there is essential agreement, with a touch of individuality and choice of words which show the testimony to be personal:

"The sky was covered with clouds and it rained much. We could not see the sun. Then suddenly, at noon, the clouds drew away and the sun appeared as if it were trembling. It seemed to come down. It began spinning like a fire-wheel in the pagan feasts. It stopped for a few minutes and again started rolling, perhaps in a diameter of more than a meter while we could look at it as though it were the moon. Things all around turned into different colors."

"Were you afraid?"

"I was afraid. I thought the sun would fall upon us."

"Were your clothes wet before, then suddenly dry?"

"Yes."

"When it was over, how did you feel?"

"I was relieved of a great fright I had felt. I resolved to lead a better life and to amend for my sins."

From thousands of witnesses who were on the mountain, we have chosen witnesses of every possible age, of every possible class, of those inclined to believe and those who were not, those who were educated scientists and those who could neither read nor write. We have withheld nothing. *We have not chosen any one particular deposition nor one particular witness over another for any reason* other than avoidance of too much repetition.

Chapter 8
THE LAWYER

Carlos de Azevedo Mendes, from Torres Novas, was a successful lawyer in the prime of life when the miracle occurred. He was twenty-eight years of age. He first went to Fatima, in September of 1917, on a horseback excursion. He explains that it was partly sport and partly curiosity that drew him to that mystery mountain towering beyond Batalha.

Being an impulsive and active man, Carlos went right to the home of the three children involved in the miracle. He talked, even played with them. He was greatly impressed by their sincerity, and deeply touched by a mysterious emotion which he could not altogether define. In his 1960 deposition he explains:

"After that first visit to Fatima in early September, I wrote a letter to my future bride telling her that I was convinced that there was something unusual about the children, and that I was going back to Fatima on the 13th of the month, when the next apparition was expected."

We interrupt Mr. Mendes' testimony here to reproduce part of the letter which his future wife fortunately saved. We begin with his description of the youngest of the three children, the seven-year-old

Carlos de Azevedo Mendes in 1915.

Mendes in 1960.

Jacinta:

"I would like to describe her features to you but I believe that I would accomplish nothing in telling you. I could only approximate them. Jacinta wore a kerchief with reddish border wrapped about her head, with ends tied behind and bringing out her features. Her black eyes were of an enchanting liveliness. She had an angelic expression of goodness which captivated me...

"After being entertained for sometime, talking and (don't laugh) playing, Francisco came in. A cap concealed his head. He wore a very short jacket, a vest which permitted his shirt to show, tight trousers—in short—a little man. A good boy's face. A bright glance and a roguish look. He answered my questions straightforwardly.

"Lucia does not have impressive features. Only her eyes are impressive. Her face is common, typical of the region. At first she was shy, but soon I had them all at ease. Then without hesitation they answered and satisfied all my curiosities... As I told you, I questioned all three separately.

"All the children say is that a Lady appears to them. They do not know who she is. Only after the sixth time, on October 13th, will she tell them who she is and what she wants... The naturalness and ingenuousness with which they told what they had seen is admirable and impressive.

"To hear the children, to see them in their simplicity, impresses us in an extraordinary manner and makes us conclude that in all they have told us there is something supernatural... Today it is my belief that there is here an extraordinary event which reason alone cannot comprehend. What is it? I await the next 13th with growing anxiety. It is certain that I had a sense of well being when I was with the children and even lost notion of time. There was an attraction which I cannot explain—to express his admiration the boy told me that the Lady was extremely beautiful. I showed him your picture and

asked: 'Is she more beautiful?' and they all replied: 'Much
more! The Lady was dressed all in white and gold!'"

Forty three years after this letter was written, in 1960, we
asked Mr. Mendes about the miracle itself. This is his account:

"There were many thousands of people at Fatima on
September 13th (the month before the miracle) and many persons claimed to see a silver rain and other phenomena, but I
saw nothing. Then suddenly the children were getting up, saying it was over. As the crowd advanced to question the children, I pressed through and took Lucia up in my arms. She
cried and said, 'Let me alone! Let me alone!'

"I felt hurt, but proceeded to deliver her to some of her family. I left Fatima absolutely disillusioned and convinced by the
attitude of the children that there was much here to question. If
they had just seen and spoken to the Mother of Heaven, I could
not understand why they cried and asked to be left alone.

"I told several people of my disillusion and publicly
declared that I would not go to Fatima on October 13th. My
brother, Augusto, a medical doctor who was home from the
war in France on leave, intended to go. But I persuaded him
not to. Another of my brothers, Candido, had promised to take
several persons to Fatima and insisted that I accompany him. I
repeatedly refused.

"Candido and I slept in the same room. At 4 A.M. I heard
him getting up to leave for Fatima. I jumped out of the bed, and
always protesting that I would not go, I went along.

"At twelve o'clock noon, without knowing how or why, I
found myself standing close to the spot of the apparition."

"There were many persons there, but I felt alone. I was suddenly dominated by the expectation of the great event which
the children had foretold so that 'Everyone might believe.' I
saw the children arrive, saw them kneel down, and was gripped
by the impressive silence which fell upon us. It is as real to me
now as it was at that moment."

We interrupted Mr. Mendes to put the following question: "Did you have any idea of what was going to happen?"

"No, I did not have the slightest idea of what might happen. But now, waiting, I did believe that the sign which the children predicted was going to take place. I heard, while the children were talking to the vision, persons around me remark about different things they saw. But I saw nothing unusual."

"What time was it that the children started to talk to the vision?"

"It might have been at solar noon,[1] or a few moments later."

"When the people began to shout, did you see anything unusual?"

"I saw the sun, as if it were a ball of fire, begin to move in the clouds. It had been raining all morning and the sky was full of clouds, but the rain had stopped. It lasted for several seconds, crushingly pressing down upon us all. Wan faces, standing here, from every side great ejaculations, acts of contrition, of the love of God. An indescribable moment! We feel it. We remain dominated by it. But it is not possible to describe it."

"What did you do, Mr. Mendes?"

"As I said, it had been raining. I was wearing a waterproof coat, waterproof trench coat. I was filled with curiosity and emotion and with the same impulse that I had felt in September, I pressed forward and took little Lucia up into my arms and put her on my shoulder.

"Now, contrary to her action on September 13th, from my shoulder, as if under the inspiration and fulfillment of an order she had received, she cried out: 'Our Lady wants the people to pray and do penance.' She said it over and over, adding, 'If this is done, the war will end.'

"My heart was filled to overflowing. I who had been hurt by the reticence of this same child a month before, now had made

---

1. This would be about one-thirty, according to the "official" time on that day.

of my shoulder a pulpit from which the great message of Fatima was announced to an awe-struck sea of witnesses. I resolved at that moment, as long as my health allowed, to work at Fatima in some useful way."

(This is a promise which Carlos Mendes has faithfully kept through the years. On every thirteenth of the month he was always to be seen in the forefront of the servants at Fatima who helped with the sick and helped to manage the great crowds. By 1960 he had built a house near the Cova to spend his last days there.)

"Did the message of Fatima and the Miracle of the Sun affect others who saw it?"

"What I saw at Fatima could not help but affect my interior life and I am sure that all who saw the Miracle, or even heard about it, cannot fail to be impressed by its greatness... I still remember it today as vividly as at the moment it happened, and I feel myself dominated by that extraordinary event seen on the 13th of October, 1917, at Fatima. I am not alone. All of Portugal has been deeply affected."

Wearing the straps of the "Servants of Fatima," Mr. Mendes accompanies the Blessed Sacrament at a Fatima ceremony.

Chapter 9
FROM ALL CLASSES

On August 1, 1917, the Baron of Alvaiazere learned of the heroism of the children of Fatima in the Ourem prison.

The Baron had not believed before, but he became a very important witness to the Miracle of the Sun. After the death of Francisco in 1919 he helped to send the dying Jacinta to Lisbon in the hope of saving her life by an operation. (The little girl prophesied that she would die and that the trip to Lisbon would be in vain. But she accepted the journey to offer the suffering in reparation for sins of the world.)

When Jacinta died, the Baron of Alvaiazere had her little body brought back to Ourem and placed in his family's tomb, where it remained until long after the Fatima apparitions had been approved by the Church. (Her body is now on the gospel side of the great Basilica of Fatima.) Among the numerous depositions which we have obtained for this book is that of the Baron's sister, Maria Celeste da Camara e Vasconcelos, who now is living on the family property in Ourem.

At the time of the miracle she was on the old road with relatives and friends overlooking the Cova.

Body of Jacinta being returned to Fatima.

Maria Celeste da
Camara e Vasconcelos

"Did you think anything might happen, Madame?" we asked.

"I expected that all was a fancy of the poor children and *that we would see nothing.*"

"What happened?"

"The sun began to spin with circles of every color. It was like a wheel of fireworks, and coming down to the ground."

"What was your reaction?"

"Stupefied."

"Did you think it a miracle?"

"Yes, there was something supernatural."

"Did you know of anyone there who did not see the miracle?"

"No."

Unfortunately these are only printed words and pictures before the reader, and they are only a few examples from thousands. But certainly the reality of the miracle begins to emerge as we patiently listen to one witness after the other... each different, yet testifying to the same incredible event which bears upon *our* avoidance of atomic war.

Seventy-one years old in 1960, José Joaquim da Assunção is living at Montelo, and at the moment of the miracle he was standing fairly close to the place of the apparitions where the fountain is now located. He was with several acquaintances. He had tried to get as good a location as possible. This is what he saw:

José Joaquim da
Assunção in 1960.

"The sun began spinning as though in a sort of a box. All the people cried: 'It comes down! It comes down!' The colors of things seemed different."

"How were you dressed, José?"

"I was not dressed in a special way. Just as usual. It was raining."

"And were you dry afterward?"

"The sun began to come down and all were quickly dried."

"What was your personal reaction?"

"In August I was more impressed than in October. In August I went to fetch some pumpkins not very far from the Cova when I heard that the children were taken to prison. I decided to go, and promised my gold watch and chain if I ever saw the vision... I was so happy, as if I really had seen her. I kept my promise."

"Did you know of anyone there who did not see the miracle?"

"I never heard that they had seen nothing. They were all obliged to see, except those who might not look at it."

We used an entire chapter for the description of the miracle by Dominic Reis of Holyoke, Massachusetts, but only a few paragraphs for many other witnesses—although all are of equal importance. This is because the largest audience of this book may be in the United States, and it is advantageous to have testimony which can be verified locally.

One witness of the miracle, now living in New York, is the Reverend Joseph Cacella. He welcomes hearing from anyone. He has distributed hundreds of thousands of leaflets about Fatima.

Still another American witness is Mr. Higino Faria, who lives in Oakland, California. In 1917 Mr. Faria lived in Olaia, seven miles from Fatima. Two days before the miracle, he says, "Caravans of people were passing in front of the house,

Mr. Higino Faria, with his daughter Hilda, photographed in his California home.

clothed in every possible fashion, many without shoes, many from distant places, like Alentejo and Algarve.

"I was sick with a severe cold and hoarseness, and I asked, 'Where are these people going?' When I learned that they were going because of a predicted miracle, even though I was sick, I wished to go. Having no other means, I went on foot. My wife was very disturbed and said, 'What are you going to do? Don't you know you are going to aggravate the state of your health?'"

Mr. Faria left his house at nine o'clock in the morning. By the time he reached the top of the mountain at Fatima: "We became victims of a heavy rain which wet our clothing and made us very cold." He then describes what he saw:

"When I arrived at eleven o'clock, I was surprised at the great number of people on the slope of the hill. Completely wet, dirty and frozen, we waited.

"At one o'clock the clouds gathered into a very thick and dark form, giving the appearance of an eclipse. At that moment I looked at the multitude and had the impression that it was the day of final judgment. The faces of the people looked thin, long and yellow. Then the dark cloud broke into parts, and through the break we saw the sun shining, spinning in the shape of a wheel of fire. It seemed to approach the earth...

"Everyone was dried, cleaned. I who was sick, returned completely cured. In thanksgiving for such a great grace and my cure, I promised to recite the Rosary every day of my life."

Another witness in America is living near Albany, but she

is reluctant to have herself known because her story was once published and she was embarrassed by the number of visitors. Her testimony is similar to all the others, but she adds: "Even today, whenever there is lightning, I remember it and I am afraid."

She, also, affirms that all the people had been wet and suddenly they were dry. She thought it was to have been the end of the world. Her affidavit will be made available to anyone with a special interest in the circumstances.

An American witness who speaks freely to any visitor is Mrs. Ermina L. Caixero, of 89 Washington Avenue, in White Plains, N.Y. She is a daily Communicant and has been back to Fatima, all the way from America, several times.

But these are only a few of the witnesses whom we have discovered. There are certainly living witnesses now to be found in any corner of the world where Portuguese have settled.

Now we have the testimony of Mario Godinho, a member of an important and distinguished Portuguese family. He decided after all these years to give his testimony after reading an appeal which we made through the newspapers in Portugal in preparation for this book. It is the first testimony we present from a man who was *completely* skeptical, and it has a surprising sequel.

Mario Godinho

An engineer from Vila do Paco, Mario Godinho went to Fatima in 1917 for a reason that has perhaps taken many persons to many unexpected events: He had an automobile and his mother and other members of the family wanted him to take them.

He did not believe that anything would happen. He did not even bother to get out of the car. He was sitting in the automobile on the road when the miracle began. The deposition he gave us in 1960 reads as follows:

"I got out of the car. I could look straight at the sun without difficulty. It was like a disc of dimmed glass illuminated from behind, moving around and around, and then gave the impression of falling down."

"Do you remember, Mr. Godinho, how you were dressed?"

"I don't remember, but it was certainly an ordinary suit."

"Was it dry afterward?"

"Yes, at the end of the miracle it got dry."

"What was your reaction?"

"I was greatly impressed."

"Do you know of anyone who did not see it?"

"No."

Thus ends the deposition of one of our many eyewitnesses... brief, objective, and revealing very little of the real reaction of the witness within himself.

But now that we have just read the "highlights" of Mario Godinho's deposition, due to one of the good fortunes experienced in preparing this book we are able to give this engineer's story in greater detail... thereby not only opening the door to the long corridors in this witness' memory, but to suggest all the unsaid things which hover about the testimony of all our other witnesses.

Godinho wrote a sequel for us in January, 1960. Shortly after he had made the deposition quoted above, he recognized what we were trying to do and after some deliberation he decided... for the first time since the miracle... to tell of his early disbelief, and of his shame:

"Now I am sixty-seven years old. At this age there are no more earthly illusions; at this age one lives with his eyes on

eternity. When Our Lady came I was twenty-five. That was the age of the illusions. It was difficult to me then to think of the supernatural world. We lived at that time in Portugal, in a difficult religious and political period.

"I live eighteen miles from Fatima. And in May of 1917 we were told about extraordinary apparitions, but the news came to us mixed up with the fantasy of the people. Naturally I did not believe. I sincerely supposed it was only imagination of someone.

"But my mother (who was a saintly woman) believed from the beginning and asked me to take her in my car to Cova da Iria on the 13th of June. By a poor and miserable road in our Peugeot (license number 2015), after many difficulties, we managed to get there. Below the road, in a depression of the ground, we saw some dozens of people. We left the car, jumped over some stones, and met the three shepherds who had lighted candles in their hands. Other people like us were waiting for the apparition. In front of the children there was a little holm-oak tree. They said that on that holm-oak Our Lady would appear.

"We talked to the children, pointed to our car parked on the road, and told them to meet us afterward there. So they did, and we took them home where we asked them many questions. I came back to my own home very disappointed and sincerely convinced that the poor children were mistaken. I dared not tell

my friends of my going to the Cova da Iria. I would have been considered a simpleton.

"So, I suppose I was the first driver to take a car to Cova da Iria. Some years later I saw my car in some

pictures about the apparitions. I would have been ashamed should anyone have discovered that I was the owner of that car, the first to go to the place of the apparitions. This is why I never told anybody what I saw. You are the first to know of my experience.

"I suppose I was also the first to take a photo of the little shepherds, and one of the first to make a formal interrogation of the little children. In later months my family and I learned other details of the apparitions from the mouth of Lucia, who spent two or three days with us, and once or twice was among persons we hired to pick olives.

"At my mother's request, I went once more to Cova da Iria in August at the time of the apparitions. Once more I came back discouraged and disappointed. But that time, something extraordinary happened. My mother, who had had a large tumor in one of her eyes for many years, was cured. The doctors who had attended her said they could not explain such a cure.

"Still, I did not believe in the apparitions.

"Finally, and again at my mother's request, I went to the Cova da Iria once more on the 13th of October. Now there were at the Cova hundreds upon hundreds of people, and many kinds of vehicles. There was general commotion.

Godinho's photograph of the children.

"In spite of what had happened to my mother, I was disappointed and did not believe in the apparitions. So I sat inside my car. Then all at once I noticed that everybody looked at the sky. Natural curiosity attracted my attention, and I got out of the car and looked at the sky, too.

"I saw in a clear area of sky (where one should not be able to stare at the sun) the very sun. It was like a disc of smoked glass illuminated behind and turning over itself, giving us the impression that it was coming down over our heads. I could then see the sun more easily than I can see the moon on a full moon night. From those hundreds of mouths I heard words of belief and of love to the Blessed Virgin. And then I believed. I was sure I had not been the victim of suggestion. I saw that sun as I never saw it again.

"Finally, as a side note I might add, that the little holm-oak was soon shredded by the faithful who went to the Cova. Among these faithful was my mother, who got some leaves of the little tree. Two of these leaves still had drops of candle grease from the candles lighted by the three seers. I had the honor of sending one of these leaves to the Holy Father through His Eminence, Cardinal Cerejeira, Patriarch of Lisbon.

"From that holm-tree I have still one leaf I carefully keep and have carried with myself in my purse for forty-two years.

"...And this is what I saw concerning the apparitions. Since then I have seen my mother, brother, father and my wife die... I am old, full of sorrow, waiting for my hour to join those who flew to God."

Dona Maria Teresa Charters

Dona Maria Teresa Charters, another prominent living witness, is from one of the most distinguished families of Leiria. She was twenty-six years of age and was in the Cova with several relatives. She had come, she explains, because if something was going to happen, "I wanted to see it with my own eyes."

"And what did you see?"

"We distinctly saw the sun, without harm to the eyes. The sun came down, turning on itself, and throwing beams of several colors."

"Were you afraid?"

"I thought we were all to die, but I was not afraid."

Augusto Pereira dos Reis

From Amoreira, we have Augusto Pereira dos Reis, who also was twenty-six years old, and was standing on the outskirts of the crowd where the Basilica now rises.

"I saw the sun coming down, spinning," he explains.

"Did you experience anything else?"

"Yes, my clothes were first wet, and then dry."

"How did you feel when it was over?"

"I felt more calm."

"Did you know of anyone who did not see it?"

"No."

"And why do you think it happened?"

"In order that we believe more that Our Lady had appeared there."

Antonio Antunes de Oliveira was thirty-two years old. He now lives in Ameixeira, and had been to the Cova even before the day of the miracle because he was a friend of the uncle of two of the children.

Antonio Antunes de Oliveira

"Did you believe that a miracle took place?"

"At first I did not believe."

"Was it raining very much?"

"Yes, it rained much. I was wet. There was a great deal of mud."

"What did you see?"

"I looked at the sun. It did not hurt my eyes... There were many people kneeling in the mud, and I was with them.

"Were you far from the children?"

"Yes, I was far from the children, and could only see them when they were taken up in the arms of some people. One of these people was Joao Machado, who had no faith."

"What else did you see?"

"I looked at the sun and saw it spinning like a disc, rolling on itself. I saw the people changing color. They were stained with the colors of the rainbow. Then the sun seemed to fall down from the sky."

"Were you afraid?"

"I was afraid that the sun would fall down as the people said that the world was going to end."

"Was everyone around you afraid?"

"They were afraid and screaming."

"And what did they say about it?"

"They said it was a miracle."

"What did you think?"

"I thought it was a great miracle."

"Did this affect your life?"

"I now go to Fatima almost every month, and continue to have always the same faith."

Another farmer who was standing in this same part of the crowd where the Basilica has been built, is Manuel Francisco. He was twenty-seven years of age and was standing in the crowd with his wife.

Manuel Francisco

"The sun began to come down until it seemed we were almost near it, and it threw beams of light. It was getting dark and all the people screamed."

"How did you feel?"

"I was so afflicted that I came home weeping."

"But what did you do immediately after the miracle?"

"I went to say some prayers close to the spot where the vision appeared, then came home."

"Were you still weeping?"

"My heart was afflicted. I could not help crying."

What kind of event could have caused a strong country farmer of the Serra d'Aire Mountains, head of a family, in the prime of his manhood, to weep?

Chapter 10
Children Set Before Them

At the center of the vast, terrified crowd, there were three children.

What did these children see?

Antonio dos Reis Novo lives near Fatima at Moimenta. He was the same age as Lucia (the eldest of the children). He remembers:

"I was near the children where I could see very well. Lucia was my age, and I was often with her tending the sheep. But I never deserved to see anything."

Antonio dos Reis Novo

"And what happened, Antonio?"

"The sun seemed to become a spin-wheel, rolling very fast and it turned to many colors—very different from usual."

"How were you dressed?"

"I was dressed something like Francisco, who was my neighbor. I also wore a long cap. He had a quick temper. His brother, Joao, was much milder."

"How did you feel when you saw the sun spinning?"

"I was filled with such faith, such enthusiasm..."

"Did you expect a miracle to happen?"

"Nobody knew anything about what might happen."

"Did that miracle influence your life?"

"Yes."

"Do you know of anyone who was converted by the Miracle?"

"Many people were converted."

"And what do you think the Miracle meant?"

"Of course, it showed the Power of God."

Another who was beside the three children is João Carreira, son of Maria da Capelinha, who played an important part in the early history of the apparitions.

In his testimony in 1960, Joao says that, with the crowd pressing from all sides, his knees were actually between the feet of Lucia and Francisco.

"Were you there just because of your mother's interest?"

"I wanted to see."

"What were you doing before the miracle started?"

"We were waiting. When the vision disappeared, Lucia told us to look at the sun."

"And what did you see?"

"I saw the sun rolling and it seemed as though it were coming down, like the wheel of a bicycle. Then it went back to its place. That's the way it seemed to me."

"Were you afraid?"

"I was not afraid. But I heard others crying out: 'Oh, we are going to die! We are going to die!,' but I was not afraid."

"Was there anything else extraordinary?"

"Our clothes were dry in a moment."

João Carreira

"What did you think was going to happen?"

"Lucia had said that a miracle would happen and we were waiting what might come, but we did not know whether it might be this or that."

"Did you ever know of anyone there who did not see the miracle?"

"I do not know anyone who says that he had not seen."

The testimony in this book is

(*Left to right*) Lucia dos Santos, Francisco and Jacinta Marto

from living witnesses. There is so much testimony that we can use it freely, and therefore there is no need to repeat testimony which has appeared previously, except that of the newspapers and of a few other "classical" or "key" witnesses.

Maria do Carmo Marques da Cruz Menezes was forty-six years old at the time of the miracle and even now she is an active housewife in her home near Leiria. She knew the children and was beside them. She gave us her description in March 1960.

Maria do Carmo Menezes

"Suddenly the sun appeared so that we could look at it as though it were the moon. It began spinning like a firework wheel, making us all turn into the colors of the rainbow, even the ground itself."

Was she wet and then dry afterward? "Yes." Was she

afraid? "No, I trusted God." Why did she think it happened? "That people might be converted, I think."

But then, seeing our desire to catch the reality of these events, Mrs. Menezes said:

"I had two of the children, Lucia and Jacinta, in my house for eight days in August, two months before the miracle. They said that there would be a miracle in order that all should believe... and this I saw, with my two sons who have now died. We saw the sun spinning like fireworks. I cried out: 'My God, how great is Your Power!'

"One day I had said to the children: 'Alas, you are mistaken. They will fry you in oil!' And they said: 'We are not afraid. She does not deceive us. She is so beautiful! Sometimes she dazzles us!'

"Other things I have witnessed since: The bombs which officials put there, and the one which was near the tree and did not explode. I held one in my hands. I saw the poison that they threw into the well.

"I also saw four cures at the place of the apparitions: Two were of tuberculosis, one of a girl from Lisbon and the other from Alfarelos; two were crippled girls."

It was Mrs. Menezes who remembers with joy that not only did two of the children spend a week in her house, but that it was she who gave them the "skirts with white spots, and a blouse and scarf, and an apron to each one" (clothing now familiar to many from photographs of the poor mountain children).

Maria dos Prazeres, a widow living near Fatima, was thirty-

Maria dos Prazeres

one years of age when the miracle took place. She still lives in the same house where she lived at the time of the apparitions, which is about an hour's walk from the place where the miracle happened.

"Were you close to the children?"

"I saw them come, and I was close enough to hear them speak and to understand everything they said."

"What happened?"

"I saw the sun turn upon itself; it seemed to fall from the sky. Near me there was a man and a lady who were looking at the sun through binoculars and who were saying that they saw a ladder near the sun and that Saint Joseph and the Child Jesus were there... The people around me were crying that the world was going to end.

"I knew that something extraordinary and mysterious had happened. I was sure that the children had spoken to someone extraordinary, who was not of this world."

She seemed particularly impressed by the fact that the children had predicted that something would happen. "Moreover," she repeated, "the little shepherds had announced in advance that there would be a miracle in October so that everyone would believe."

José Joaquim da Silva

Another who was close enough to hear the children was José Joaquim da Silva. He says that it was raining, there was a great deal of mud, and that he was "soaked." He saw the children kneeling in front of the tree, staring at someone unseen, and: "I heard them speaking."

"What happened?"

"We could look at the sun without

difficulty, the sky became clear... I was not afraid but I thought that there was something extraordinary. Persons around me who were seeing something extraordinary, cried with fear.[1] They were saying that the world was going to end."

"What was your personal reaction?"

"I had the conviction that the children were not mistaken, and that we were not mistaken either. I thought that God had, on that day, caused many people to see something extraordinary."

Another close to the children was Joaquim da Silva Jorge, who had joined the great crowd on the six hour trek through the rain that October 13th from Leiria to the top of the mountain. At the time of his recent statement to us in 1960, he was a retired farmer of eighty years. He already was approaching middle age on that eventful day in 1917 when he pushed through the crowd to a place near the children.

Joaquim da Silva Jorge

"I saw a dark cloud coming from the sky and then there opened a firework of sun that was coming from the East," he testifies. "Suddenly the ground was blue."

---

1. José da Silva did not see the sun fall from the sky, as is evident from the fact that he was not afraid and others around him were crying in fear because they saw something extraordinary which he did not see. He had looked at the sun but then was looking at the children and the crowd. His description of the general reaction of the crowd and the fact that he was able to look at the sun without harm to his eyes, makes his testimony particularly impressive—because he feels that, despite all this he actually did not see the miracle. In the rather thorough investigations made for this book, he was one of only two persons we found who thought they had not seen the miracle, although some others realized that they did not see the sun fall from the sky because they were looking elsewhere during that terrible moment (as was the case with Dominic Reis).

"What did you do during the miracle?"

"I stood looking at the unbeliever. (This would be Mr. Mendes—whose story is told in chapter eight. Clothed in a trench coat and peaked cap, some might have taken Mendes to be associated with the government and hence "an unbeliever.") He took one of the children who predicted the miracle into his arms and was running away, I don't know where. I had my eyes wide open trying to see the vision."[2]

"Did you experience anything else?"

"I was all wet, and afterward my clothes were quite dry."

"Did you expect this miracle to happen?"

"No, I expected something, but I didn't know what."

"Were you afraid?"

"I thought it was the end of the world."

"What effect did it have on you?"

"My faith increased. I visited, and still visit very often, the place of the apparitions."

"Do you know of anyone who did not see it?"

"I don't. Everyone has seen."

Since the compiler of these simple testimonials is perhaps the only living American layman privileged to have talked with the child who predicted the miracle, it is only fitting that we close this chapter with a description of what the children actually saw... through the testimony of the one who is still living.

Although their families had come to protect them (because generally it was felt that the children would suffer bodily harm—either from the soldiers before the time of the miracle—or from the crowd if the miracle did not come as predicted), the children were not afraid. They were confident that their vision would come, and that she would keep her promise

---

2. Apparently he means that although he was looking at Lucia he was at the same time, trying to see the entire area.

This is Sister Lucia as the writer saw her on October 18, 1952, and described her to James Ramsey Hunt, *SOUL Magazine* staff artist.

and perform a miracle.

During an interview with Lucia in 1946, the author presented a picture of the Miracle of the Sun prepared by an artist. He hoped that she would be able to confirm that the picture was what she had seen, or describe in what way the picture differed from the reality.

He made the following notes on the back of the picture as she talked:

Suddenly the vision rose from the top of the tree with light streaming from her hands... the light reflected back from the sky, much stronger than the sun.

Figures in light appeared—Our Lady as she had always appeared to us—Saint Joseph holding the Infant in light with Our Lady, both Saint Joseph and the Infant blessing the crowd...

The light changes and suddenly Our Lady becomes Our Lady of Sorrows... Saint Joseph is replaced by Our Lord and Our Lord blesses the crowd... and then the light changes again and Our Lady becomes Our Lady of Mount Carmel while Our

Lord remains. The light fades. We hear people shouting.

"I think that what the people saw had been a reflection of the brilliance of the vision," she explained.

Immediately she was filled with an overwhelming desire to tell all the world that war is a punishment for sins and that men must do penance and cease offending God because He is so much offended.

She remembers that a man suddenly picked her up and put her on his shoulder. She took advantage of this position to shout to all the people:

"You must pray and do penance!"

In this moment she was quite different from the child who, during the previous months, had always tried to run and hide from the crowds of people who pressed to see her and her cousins.

After October 13, 1917, she once again became a shy, reticent child—afflicted by the publicity, saddened by the prophecy that Francisco and Jacinta would soon die and she would be left alone.

Today, in the peace and security of a Carmelite Convent (where the writer again was privileged to see her face in 1955), she is childlike, humble. She believes that the world is slow in accepting the "Message from Heaven."

Chapter 11
THE UNWILLING WITNESS

Two prominent newspapers of Portugal at that time were *Diario de Noticias* ("The Daily News") and *O Século* ("The Century"). Both were predominantly anti-religious. Even after the reports we are about to quote, these papers returned to attacks upon religion and specifically upon the events of Fatima.

There... cold and real and black on white... in the editions from October 13th to October 17th, these newspapers have recorded eye witness accounts of editors and reporters who had been at Fatima. They had expected to report a crowd dispersed and put to flight by soldiers, or a crowd repudiating the children because a miracle predicted had not materialized.

But this—verbatim—is what they saw... as they wrote it and as it appeared in print in *Diario de Noticias*:

"The rains kept falling. Drops trickled down the women's skirts of coarse wool or striped cotton, making them as heavy as lead. Water dripped from the caps and broadbrimmed hats onto Sunday finery. Bare feet of women and hobnailed boots of men sloshed in the wide pools of muddy roads. They did not seem to notice the rain but went up hills without stopping, illuminated by faith, anxious for sight of the miracle promised by the lady to take place at noon.

"A murmur drifting down from the hills reached us. It was a murmur like the faraway voice of the sea. It was the religious songs, now becoming clear, intoned by thousands of voices. On the plateau, over a hill, filling the valley, there was a vast and a moving mass of thousands upon thousands of people in prayer."

O Século adds that, entering Fatima, some of those who had become atheists during the seven years of the atheist regime were joking. "Aren't you going to see the saint?" one asked. "Not unless she comes to see me!" and the newspaper continues:

"They laughed heartily but the devout went on, indifferent to anything which was not part of their pilgrimage. All night long through the dark and rain, the most varied vehicles moved into the town square (of Ourem) carrying the faithful and the curious, and also old ladies, somberly dressed and weighted by the years.

"At dawn the sun was rising grayly through the rain but dark clouds loomed over Fatima. Yet nothing could stop the crowd converging from every road toward that now holy place.

"Though some came in luxurious automobiles, continually sounding their horns, oxcarts dragged slowly alongside them. There were carriages of all types, victoria chaises, landaus, and wagons fitted out for the occasion with seats and crowded to the limit."

After a further description of the vehicles and the people, *O Século* continues:

"About ten o'clock in the morning the skies were altogether black and sheets of rain, driven by a chilly northeast wind, whipped the faces of the pilgrims, drenched the roads, and chilled the people to the bone. Some sought shelter under the trees, against the walls, or in scattered houses. Parked along the road near Fatima were carriages of every type and thousands of pilgrims that had come from many miles around and from the provinces, gathered about the small oak tree which, in the words of the children, their Lady had chosen as a pedestal. This small, shredded tree was the center of a great circle around which the devout and other spectators ranged themselves."

Then, in the Cova da Iria, *Diario de Noticias* reports:

"At one o'clock the rain stopped. The sky had a certain gray clarity but seemed to suddenly be getting darker. The

sun seemed veiled in gauze. We could look at it without strain. The gray tint of mother-of-pearl began changing as if into a silver disc that was growing and growing... until it broke the clouds! Then the silvery sun, still shrouded in that grayish light, began to rotate and wander within the circle of the receded clouds!

"The people cried out with one voice. Thousands, transported by ecstasy fell to their knees upon the muddy ground. Then, as if it were shining through the stained glass windows of a great cathedral, the light became a rare blue, spreading its rays upon the nave... Slowly the blue faded away and now the light seemed to be filtered through yellow. Yellow spots were falling now upon the white kerchiefs and dark shirts of coarse wool. They were spots which repeated themselves indefinitely over the landscape. All the people were weeping and praying bareheaded, weighted down by the greatness of the miracle. These were seconds, moments, that seemed hours..."

O Século, the other heretofore skeptical newspaper adds:

"From beside the parked carriages and where many thousands stood, afraid to descend into the muddy soil of the Cova da Iria, we saw the immense crowd turn toward the sun at its highest, free of all clouds. The sun seemed to us like a plate of dull silver. It could be seen without the least effort. It did not blind or burn. It seemed as though an eclipse were taking place. All of a sudden a tremendous shout burst forth, 'Miracle, miracle!'

"Before the astonished eyes of the people, whose attitude carried us back to Biblical times, and who, white with terror, heads uncovered, gazed at the sun which trembled and made brusque and unheard of movement beyond all cosmic laws, the sun seemed literally to dance in the sky.

"Immediately afterward the people asked each other if they

saw anything and what they had seen. The greatest number avowed that they saw the sun trembling and dancing; others declared they saw the smiling face of the Blessed Virgin herself. They swore that the sun turned around on itself as if it were a wheel of fireworks and had fallen almost to the point of burning the earth with its rays. Some said they saw it change colors successively."

The reporter from *O Século* was Avelino de Almeida, who went to school with the president of the Municipal Council of Santarem, Antonio de Bastos. Mr. de Bastos was among the many unbelievers who had gone to Fatima. He decided to write Almeida, after reading the report in *O Século*, to ask Almeida's *secret* and *personal* opinion of the phenomenon.

At the request of Bastos, Almeida wrote a much more sincere and detailed account than he had dared to give in the pages of *O Século*. It reads in part:

"Breaking a silence of more than twenty years, you write to ask me for details of what I saw and heard on the mountain at Fatima.

"Some are convinced that promises from Heaven were fulfilled; others find themselves far from believing in the unquestioned reality of a miracle. You were a believer in your youth and later ceased to be a believer. Family reasons brought you to Fatima in the great wave of people who gathered there on October 13th. Your rationalism suffered a formidable blow, and wishing to establish a definite opinion, you make use of unprejudiced evidence, such as mine, since I was there only in fulfillment of a very difficult mission, that of reporting impartially for O Século facts which might develop before me.

"It may not satisfy you, but certainly what your eyes saw and what you heard was no different from what I saw and heard, and there were few who were insensible to the grandeur

of this spectacle, unique and worthy of thought and study from every viewpoint."

And then Dr. Almeida goes on to tell, not so much from the reports of others (as he does in the reporting in *O Século*) but from his own background and observations, exactly what happened.

This testimony is extremely lengthy and we need not repeat it. However, Dr. Almeida explains that phenomena reported before October at Fatima, and historical conditions in Portugal, were responsible for this tremendous wave of

people that went to the mountain top that celebrated Saturday.

He concludes:

"Was it a miracle, as the people shouted? Was it a natural phenomenon as the learned say? I now don't care to know. But I only tell you what I saw. The rest is with science and the Church."[1]

---

1. This letter appeared in *Ilustração Portuguesa*, Number 610, October 29, 1917.1.

Chapter 12
Reality Emerges

All this testimony, taken at different times, in different places, and with a certainty of no collaboration among the witnesses, reveals only two variations:

First, *a few were not afraid*; second, *some saw more than others.*

For the first variation there is the simple fact that some persons are not afraid of death. Teresa Charters, for example, says: "I thought it was the end of the world, but I was not afraid." By contrast, some were so terrified that they lost their senses.

For the second, we could not expect everyone to have seen everything. Those ten minutes were filled with such distraction that it is remarkable that, of the many thousands of witnesses, so few missed so little. If one can try to take the place of the witnesses, the following questions could be put to oneself:

When I saw the sun had changed, would I have kept watching it, or would I... if I had expected to see the Vision which the children had been seeing... keep my eyes glued on the spot above the tree where the apparitions had been taking place?

If I had a beloved parent or child, and people were shouting that the world was going to end, would I have looked up or would I have looked in concern as to how I might protect my loved ones?

ALL testify to having witnessed something inexplicable. There is *not a single exception* to this among all the persons who have been questioned either in our survey of 1960, or during all the forty-three years preceding that survey.

In the summary from all witnesses we know that there was a four-fold wonder:

(1) The crowd looked without the aid of dark glasses or other protection upon a brilliance which they took to be the sun; (2) it emitted rays of brilliant color, which actually colored objects

on the earth; (3) it fell toward the crowd; (4) within a few minutes the area which had been wet was dry.

ALL witnessed or experienced some part of this. And it seems evident that the few who did not witness all four elements were distracted. Albano Barros, for example, in a field near Minde, was so overcome that after the light fell earthwards he does not remember what he did. He does not remember even that it had rained. He was overcome by the common fear:

Almost everyone in the area thought it was the end of the world.

Perhaps this phenomenon can be classified partly as an "astronomical" miracle (to use the classification of Leuret and Bon). In this regard it is the third such miracle in history in category, but still unique, and "first" in nature. The other two astronomical miracles were the prolongation of daylight at the prayer of Joshuah (Joshuah 10), and the sign which Ezekiel obtained for the King of Judah in 714 B.C., causing the shadow of a sundial to retrace ten hours (Kings IV, 20).

The *most* unique element in the Miracle of the Sun at Fatima is that *it was predicted in advance.*

It was predicted three times, during three consecutive months, so that some one hundred thousand witnesses gathered to see if it would really come about. It produced, in sequence, emotions of terror and relief; to merely visible phenomena was added the sudden, tangible cleansing and drying of the crowd and of the surrounding water-laden area.

Various scientific suggestions have been offered as to just WHAT the Miracle of the Sun at Fatima could have been. None satisfy. Doctor Francois Leuret and Doctor Henri Bon[1] suggest that the "Great Miracle" of Fatima was achieved by the rays of the sun, or "refraction of the rays through the

---

1. *The Modern Miraculous Cures*, by Doctor Francois Leuret and Doctor Henri Bon.

atmosphere." But the light could not have been seen through a mist because the e*dges of the phenomenon were distinct.* And there followed an *earthward* fall which caused witnesses to think it was the end of the world.

In the case of the other two astronomical miracles of history (the sundial shadow retraced and the prolongation of daylight) the nature of each miracle is not difficult to suggest.

Explanation of the "stopping of the sun" by Joshuah finds its key in the Bible itself. This manner of speaking is a poetic expression of the phenomenon: "The Lord cast down upon them great stones from heaven as far as Zeca." The miracle probably consisted of a very heavy, unexpected storm accompanied by great blocks of hail reaping more victims among the enemy than the Israelite swords.

But others explain this same Old Testament "Miracle of the Sun" by comparing it to a phenomenon which occurred in Siberia on the 30th of June, 1908. Aerolites, falling from the Siberian sky, devastated a forest over a radius of fifteen miles. There followed a "night light" which could have given the impression that the sun had lingered in the sky if it occurred at time of sunset. The combination of falling aerolites, plus the light, would seem adequately to describe the phenomenon on the Israelite battlefield.

Finally, as Doctors Leuret and Bon point out, there is the simple possibility that by Divine intervention a reflection of the sun's rays could have been produced in the upper strata of the atmosphere so that the light and appearance of the sun was still visible from the battlefield.

But for the miracle of Fatima... predicted four months before by three ignorant children... there seems no explanation whatever.

For every explanation so far offered, some contradictory factor renders the explanation invalid.

There is little we can say, therefore, about the *nature* of the miracle, although some scientific opinion is given in our foreword.

What IS to be stressed is the fact that this miracle indubitably happened. It was witnessed by *thousands*.

Twelve persons would be sufficient on a jury to determine whether a man should live or die, but Doctor Garrett counted over one hundred thousand.

These are OUR witnesses. Many live now. The message of which the miracle speaks is for *this hour*. Even the final part was not to be revealed until 1960—which was just about the time that the reality of the miracle would begin to penetrate into the consciousness of a non-miraculous minded world.[2]

What did the Church say about all this? What effect has it had, and what effect is it expected to have upon the world? After deepening our realization of the event by running over the testimony of a few more 1960 witnesses, we shall probe the mystery of Fatima more deeply.

---

2.   The final part of the message of Fatima was "secret" until 1960, at which time a sealed envelope... containing the secret... was opened by Pope John XXIII. It was not made public.

Chapter 13
RED STAR STRIKES BACK

Less than twenty years after the Miracle of the Sun, Communism struck back on the Iberian Peninsula causing... just across the Portuguese border... one of the bloodiest civil wars in history.

But while there were two million casualties in Spain, revulsion at Red excesses and the miracle of Fatima combined to help Salazar keep Portugal out of the bloodshed and Communist agitation.

However, Communism is not finished with Portugal, any more than it is finished with the rest of the world... including the United States. As the message of Fatima foretold, this atheist movement coming from Russia is bent on domination of the entire world: "Errors from atheist Russia will spread through the entire world.. fomenting wars... several entire nations will be annihilated."

Unsuccessful in getting a foot back into continental Portugal, the Communists began to concentrate on her overseas territory.

The Miracle of the Sun was obviously intended by God to *awaken* the world to the danger of Communism. Today, more than ever, we can realize why: It is often a hidden danger, under a cloak of righteousness, which seeks to divide and conquer the world before its true purpose and power are evident. Cubas of the world are to become continents, and the ensuing slavery of men's souls might make the ages of earliest barbarism seem like days of spiritual enlightenment.

But Portugal could remember the great "Reds" of 1917... who boasted that they would make that nation atheist within two generations. The Portuguese could remember that Lisbon was designated by the Soviets as the "Atheist Capital of the World" ...before Moscow had even heard of the Soviets. And they could remember how these same men disappeared... how they died... And while fearing their Soviet successors, who have developed armed might in Russia and Asia... holding in their atomic arsenals the very power of the sun itself... they remember a greater power that, commanded by the prayer of three children, appeared in the sun over the mountain at Fatima. They remember the promise of the message of Fatima: If enough people turn to God, as Our Lady of Fatima request-ed, *the hearts of the Communist leaders will be changed.*

This does not mean, of course, that the social evils in the world... which Communism promises to cure... will be simulta-neously solved. It means that the solution of the injustices of the world must be accomplished voluntarily, out of love of God and of men created in His Image. It means that the solution offered by the Soviet is an illusion... a hideous moral deformity cloaked in the offer of liberation from poverty which gives instead the worst of all slaveries: the slavery of the spirit.

The situation is complex, and we could argue for days on end... as happens in the United Nations over one world trouble spot after the other... on the sins and virtues of various politi-cal sides.

Father de Vos, Missionary in the Congo, was killed by Communists in the Congo in the Spring of 1961 because of a Mass of reparation said for the desecration by the Communists of an image of Our Lady of Fatima. They cut off his ears, gouged out his eyes, cut off his head and then dismembered his body.

Perhaps that is why the Miracle of the Sun was so necessary.

If we look at Cuba, we remember that in the United States there was sympathy for the Castro rebels when... with small forces... they took over the country. After all, it was generally known in America that Batista had not done much to alleviate the poverty of Cuban peasants, and there was graft and political corruption. Castro promised to eliminate the graft and give social justice.

This is the picture of Communist expansion everywhere. It conquers while we are confused over social or other evils. And when we attack the individual Communist aggression such as the piracy of the *Santa Maria* and massacres in Angola, for instance, it can be argued on the other side that there are no labor unions in Portugal; that the elections are not "free." And while we argue, the pirates are acquitted, and instead of Communists being denounced for the Angola massacres (which still have to be "proved") world opinion begins to move against the Portuguese government which has been one of the most unrelenting foes of the Soviet.

The dramatic miracle in Portugal (and we use the Portuguese conflict with Communism to illustrate it) *lifts our attention from the social conflict in the world to GOD.*

This message certainly does not condone social injustice. It does not speak of government. Not even the Soviet or Communism is mentioned in the message of Fatima, but only that: "*Error* will spread from an *atheist* Russia."

The message of Fatima, confirmed by the Miracle of the Sun, says that the revolution spreading from Russia through the world is NOT THE SOLUTION to the world's injustices, and that on the other hand it is a danger so great that it will lead to the *annihilation* of entire nations if we don't recognize it for what it is and *turn to God.* The Miracle of the Sun says that, while we are distracted by the social conflict of nations, the powers of Hell through the Soviet are taking over the world—bit by bit.

It is not our purpose here to analyze the current world struggle profoundly. It is our purpose merely to awaken realization that GOD HAS INTERVENED in this crucial struggle.

In Guatemala, where Communism *almost* took power before it did so in Cuba, one of the Bishops issued a directive to all pastors to establish the Blue Army of Our Lady of Fatima (a spiritual movement whose members promise to fulfill the conditions of the message of Fatima for the conversion of Russia). In this message the Bishop (Most Rev. Constantino Luna) said:

"Knowing that only spiritual forces can crush materialism and Communism, and having asked God for light and having sought consolation from the 'Consoler of the Afflicted,' we have taken the decision to unite ourselves with those who have responded to the demands of Our Lady of Fatima to bring about fulfillment of what she promised: "Russia will be converted and there will be peace."'...We cannot live with illusions... The hour through which the world is passing is grave; grave and dangerous. At stake is the very purpose of people in the world, of the eternal destiny of each man created in the Image of God. Today to organize programs and to spend time in discussions is to lose time uselessly. The time for action has arrived... firm, constant action, so intense that God will turn again to us. Let it be a spiritual action... an unconditional obedience to the appeal of the Virgin, our Patroness, who says at Fatima: "If my requests are heard, Russia will be converted..."

Only on faith can we accept such a solution to the world problem.

Was that not why the Miracle of the Sun took place? So, as the children foretold, and as every witness agrees... *everyone may believe?*

If there is a quick and easy solution to the economic and social ills of the world, we have not yet found it. Progress against disease and poverty is being made every day. But at the same time we have retrogressed to a spiritual debasement because of, or in competition with, materialistic Communism.

Accelerated by the cataclysms of two world wars, in the confusion caused by the sudden merging of disparate nations and cultures into "one world," Communism is snaking its way to world power... stealthily, silently, little by little, but fatally.

While there is open red-star bloodshed in Guatemala, there is camouflaged bloodshed in Cuba... and Cuba falls. While there is an ostensible move in any one place (Berlin, Korea, Lebanon, etc.), *there is a successful hidden move* some place else.

Ever present is the danger that the fangs of the snake are a deadly poison that kills men's souls. Children are taken from parents and sent to schools to learn that there is no God, that they are animals. Older persons who cannot be "taught" atheism are isolated, turned to slave labor, or killed. And also present is the realization that if we turn upon this snake too suddenly, to club it, it can rear up with atomic power and destroy us all.

The message of Fatima... confirmed by the Miracle of the Sun: Turn to God, and He will change the snake into a dove.

Chapter 14
MORE WITNESSES

"What happened here on October 13, 1917?" we asked Antonio Rosa, on his Casa Velha farm, near Fatima. "The miracle happened," the Portuguese farmer answered simply.

Antonio Rosa

He had gone to the place of the apparitions with Manuel dos Santos, brother of one of the children who saw the "visions."

"How did you feel during the miracle, Antonio?"

"Rather disturbed," he answered, "it caused me to kneel down... as soon as possible we got the children together and ran back home."

Joseph Frazao, also from the same area, told us on February 11, 1960:

"The sky was covered with clouds but suddenly the clouds opened. The sun seemed to be coming down from the sky and looked like a wheel of fireworks, shooting off all colors of the rainbow.

Joseph Frazao

"Did you have any idea that something like this might happen?"

"No."

Another farmer from Fatima is Antonio Da Silva Reis, who was twenty-nine years of age. He said he had gone only out of curiosity.

"What did you see, Antonio?"

"The sun turned on itself."

"What was your reaction?"

"Surprised, even frightened."

"How long do you think it lasted?"

"Ten or fifteen minutes."

"And how did you feel afterward?"

"I began to talk to others about it. We were still frightened."

"Do you know of anyone who was there but did not see the miracle?"

"No."

Maria Guerra was only a child at the time, but she remembers it as though it were yesterday. She had come to the Cova in order to help her uncle, who was crippled. They lived in Leiria.

"What happened?" we asked her on February 20, 1960. "Lightning opened the clouds and the sun began to tremble."

"And how did you feel, Maria?"

"Shivering and frightened."

"Do you know of anyone who was there who did not see the miracle?"

"As far as I know, they all saw."

"And you still remember it today?"

"Yes, I remember, I remember, and very well."

"And why do you think the miracle happened?"

"So that I would believe."

Maria Candida da Silva, also from Leiria, was thirty-one years of age at the time. She was in the Cova with a group of friends.

"It was raining much," she tells us in a 1960 deposition, "and all the people cried out that there would be no miracle because so much time passed and nothing happened. But the little shepherds said: 'Wait, wait a little more.' Then suddenly the rain

Maria Candida da Silva

stopped and a great splendor appeared and the children cried out: 'Look at the sun!' I saw the sun coming down, feeling that it was falling to the ground. At that moment I collapsed, and when I awoke all was over."

"Did you observe anything when you recovered consciousness?"

"My clothes had been wet because it rained much, but quickly I was dry."

"When did it happen?"

"At noon, by the sun."

"What time did it end?"

"I do not remember, because I collapsed."

"What did you do immediately afterward?"

"I was very much upset and went quickly home."

"Did you think it was the end of the world?"

"I collapsed because of the affliction."

"Has it had any effect on your life?"

"I always keep thinking about the *sign*."

"Do you know of anyone who was there but did not see it?"

"No, they all had seen."

"Have you told this to anyone who wasn't there?"

"Of course. I told everyone, and still do."

Manuel Antonio Rainho is a farmer from Amoreira; he was twenty-five years old on the day of the miracle. However, he did not go near the site of the apparitions, but stood rather high up on the edge of the Cova.

In 1960 we asked the usual question: What had he seen? "I saw the sun getting dark and

Manuel Antonio Rainho

descending toward the tree. The sun became of several colors...
It was wet, and after this it became dry."

"Why do you think it happened?"

"To prove that it was something from 'above'."

"Did you tell others about it?"

"Yes, and they were astonished."

Maria José Monteiro was seventy years of age when we
obtained her deposition in 1960, living in Leiria. She was
twenty-seven years of age at the time of the miracle. She was
near the children with some acquaintances.

"Were you afraid?" we asked her, after she had described
the "falling sun."

"Much impressed, but not afraid."

"And what else did you experience?"

"Although very wet before, I was dry afterward."

"How long do you think it lasted?"

"Perhaps some ten minutes."

"Do you remember it well?"

"Yes, as if it were today."

"Why do you think it happened?"

"To confirm the apparitions and to demonstrate the power of
God."

From the village of Chainca, Julio Vicente gave us his deposition on February 16, 1960. He was standing on the north
side of the Cova, on the outskirts of the crowd.

"I saw the sun turning very quickly and changing with several colors, and then coming down. We looked at it as though
it were the moon."

"How did you feel?"

"I felt a great emotion."

"Did you experience anything else?"

"My clothes were wet, but suddenly they dried."

"Did you have any idea of what might happen?"

"No."

"When did it happen and how long did it last?"

"About noon, and it lasted ten to fifteen minutes."

"How did you feel?"

"Somewhat frightened."

"Does it still seem real to you?"

"I remember everything as if I was seeing it in this moment."

Also from Chainca we have Joaquim Vicente, a quarry man who was twenty-two years old when the miracle happened. He was standing very close to the spot of the apparitions with his wife. He had come out of curiosity, and was standing with his umbrella over himself and his wife as protection against the rain.

In his deposition of February 16, 1960, he tells us:

"It was raining. Suddenly the clouds opened and the sun seemed as though through a window. It began spinning, coming so low that I looked at my watch and believed it was not right as the sun was so low. The sun was spinning and there were clouds of different colors like those of the rainbow. Near me a man fell on his knees and exclaimed, 'My God, forgive me.' And my wife asked me: 'So now you don't believe?' I answered: 'If the Church approves, I will believe.'"

Joaquim Vicente

"Did you experience anything else?"

"My clothes were wet, and then, without noticing it, they were dry."

"And when did it happen and how long did it last?"

"Half an hour after noon, and

lasted about ten minutes."

Like most of the residents of the small village of Fatima, Manuel da Silva was one of those who heard about the events of Fatima from the very beginning, which would be precisely six months before the miracle. He was eighteen when the miracle happened.

Manuel da Silva

Did he believe that the children were actually seeing a visitor from Heaven? From the very beginning?

"At first I felt confused. But soon I did believe in it. We know that with God nothing is impossible."

"Did you ever make fun of the children as some did?"

"No, I never did."

"What happened on October 13th?"

"I came from the direction of the parish church toward the Cova. I was alone, because I feel that when one is alone one can see things better. That morning I had to go to the city (Ourem) to obtain some merchandise for my father's business. It was raining much. It had been raining all morning."

"And what happened?"

"Shortly after I arrived, the rain stopped, the clouds began to open and the sun shone clearly and moved. I looked at it, but I couldn't stand it long."

"Did you fall on your knees?"

"No. I held myself up but there were others who threw themselves on their knees and cried and prayed."

"Where were you standing?"

"Not too far from the children. Perhaps the place where

there is now the fountain." (This would be about one hundred feet from the place of the apparitions.)

"Did you think it was the end of the world?"

"Yes."

A carpenter from Chainca, Antonio Marques, was standing more or less on the outskirts of the crowd, where the stairs of the basilica now rise on the north side of the Cova. He was with his mother, one of his brothers, and many other persons. He was trying to get down closer to the tree when it happened:

"The sky was covered with clouds, but suddenly the clouds tore away and the sun appeared as if trembling. It seemed to come down, gave a great heave, began rolling in a circle of perhaps more than a meter. It stopped, and then spun and then spun again, as though it were a wheel of fireworks, coloring everything with various colors. And we could look at it as we do the moon."

"How did you feel?"

"Frightened."

He goes on to testify in a deposition on February 16, 1960, that it lasted about ten minutes. He had fallen to his knees and was praying.

"And what was your reaction?"

"I was happy, when it was over, to have escaped that danger."

Chapter 15
Incredulous Clergy

Early books on Fatima did not detail descriptions given by many individual witnesses because many simply corroborated what had been described in the newspapers. Even when we were gathering testimony for this book, witnesses would say: "It was just as in the newspapers."

But only from individual testimony does the *reality* of the miracle emerge. We get the *impression from real persons* of a real event—which affects our world, now. Some of these witnesses are now approaching death and their depositions are beyond doubt.

Moreover, we get a more accurate impression of *the extent of the crowd* and of the *awesomeness of the miracle* as we add up the individual reactions and consider the great area over which these various witnesses were gathered.

Many reports of the time of the apparition speak of a "priest" standing near the children, who had been there all morning waiting for the time when the children arrived. As soon as the children came he asked: "When will the vision come?" The children answered that the vision would come soon. Some time passed and the "priest" cried to those around him that it was obviously a fraud. He tried forcibly to get the children to leave the spot, but was restrained by the crowd which was pressing in from all sides.

No one whom we interrogated has ever been able to identify this "priest." Perhaps he was an agent of the government dressed in clerical garb to confuse the children.

However, unknown and unrecognized by the majority of the crowd, there were priests present, like Dr. Formigao, who had spoken twice to the children at length before this day, and who was beginning to believe that they were truly having visions. Another was Father João Gomes Menitra, and his deposition was obtained by us in 1960:

*I was living at Reguengo do
Fetal, he tells us, about seven
miles from Fatima, with my parents. The day before the miracle
two couples arrived from Orti-
gosa looking for a place to
spend the night. My father invited them in and also took care of
their cart and horse.*

*After I said Mass on that
October 13th, the two ladies
invited me to go to Fatima with
them. I refused at first, but they*

Father João Menitra

*insisted so much that I decided to go, even though I did not
believe in the apparitions. I used to go and say Mass at the
Fatima church, but never once did I go to the place where the
children claimed to be seeing the visions, although I passed
there on the road every Sunday.*

*On the way up the mountain from Reguengo there were
many people on the road—on foot, in carriage, or on bicycles.
It was raining, but no one seemed to think of turning back.*

*When we had gotten fairly well up the mountain, the car-
riage was left and the two couples went down near the place
where the children would be, but I remained up near the road,
on the outside of the Cova. I was alone. Only the horse and
carriage were beside me. I remember thinking that if it rained
too much I would get under the carriage. It was about noon
when a man from Alentejo came up to me and said: 'In about
a half an hour.'*

'You know more than I do,' I answered.

*But about a quarter of an hour later the people nearest the
tree started crying out. Surprised, I looked and saw that the
people were in various colors—yellow, white, blue. At the*

same time I beheld the sun spinning at great speed and very near me. I at once thought: 'I am going to die!'

I knelt down on some stones and raised my hand, begging the pardon of God for every fault I might have committed.

A few moments later the sun ceased to spin and went back into its place. I looked at the place and saw a truck beside me in which a man in an overcoat stood crying aloud the words of the creed. And I told myself that I was not the only one to be afflicted...

We also have the deposition of Father Manuel Pereira da Silva, who had not believed in the vision.

Father da Silva points out that the "sun appeared with its circumference well defined." (Many of the witnesses mention this very clear definition of the edges of the sun, often likening it to the appearance of the sun in eclipse. It is one of the facts noted with other explicit references to the sudden clarity of the atmosphere. This is important; it shows that the phenomenon was not the appearance of the sun through moisture or fog.)

"It came down as if to the height of the clouds and began to whirl upon itself," Father da Silva testifies. "The crowd looked yellow, and most people knelt down, even in the mud..."

Dr. Manuel Formigao, a professor at the seminary and high school in Santarem (which is about half-way between Lisbon and Fatima), had been in Fatima several times after September 13th and was present at the Miracle of the Sun as a quasi-official observer.

He was one of three learned priests later appointed to the official commission of inquiry into the events of Fatima. His detailed interrogations of the children convinced him at an early stage that they were sincere. Many of the books on Fatima today report these interrogations by Dr. Formigao in detail.

He asked questions throughout the whole area before the

time of the Miracle of the Sun, as well as afterward. His testimony is similar to other testimony already given in these pages. Since he died recently we will not repeat his description of the miracle because it is repetitious and outside our purpose of viewing the miracle primarily through living witnesses.

The Pastor at Fatima shared the suspicions of most of the clergy. He refused to go to the Cova on the day of the miracle, and remained cooly aloof.

Chapter 16
THE CHURCH DECIDES

The early attitude of the Church authorities to the Miracle was so skeptical as to seem, at least to many, almost antagonistic.

The Archbishop of Mitilene, who was then the head of the Lisbon Patriarchate, sent orders to the Church authorities in the area of Fatima (and specifically to the Archpriest of Ourem and to the Vicar of Porto de Mos) ordering them to make detailed investigations. One of the reports of these investigations was sent to the Patriarchate on November 11th, and the letter accompanying the report reads as follows:

"Many persons were consulted about the affair and all of them attest to the same things which unquestionable witnesses of this document affirm, and for this reason we refrain from ordering them all to write their depositions."

Following this is a single summary of the miracle from the declarations of eye-witnesses made under sacred oath, with a long list of the names of those who testified.

Even when the Patriarchate had this evidence, it maintained a total silence in the matter. Apparently the investigations were taken merely to determine whether the Patriarchate should condemn the stories of Fatima or not.

Then in 1920, Father José da Silva, a professor at the Seminary in Porto and one of the most respected members of the Portuguese Clergy, was made Bishop of Leiria, the diocese in which Fatima is located. There had not been a Bishop in this diocese in about forty years, and everyone seemed to know that the newly appointed Bishop was to make a thorough investigation.

Were we not writing specifically about the Miracle of the Sun, we would be greatly tempted here to go into some details about this prudent Bishop and how he dealt with the message of Fatima after that August 5, 1920. He arrived in Leiria to assume the difficult task of being "Bishop of Fatima" with threats against his life and explosion of bombs in his path.

The instructions he then gave to Lucia, who was the only survivor of the three children who had predicted the miracle, might suggest that he was hostile. But looking into those gentle eyes, Lucia knew that the Bishop was acting with a controlled neutrality which fell like a two thousand year-old mantle upon this Priest, José Alves Correia da Silva, when he received the authority of the first twelve Apostles at the moment of episcopal consecration.

On May 3, 1922, almost five years after the Miracle of the Sun, the first intimation of how the Church felt was given when the Bishop publicly *nominated a commission to study* the events at Fatima: To hear everyone who might wish to testify *"either for or against in the most complete liberty."*

As we have said, many inquiries had already been made. But this was now *official*. And such an official inquiry would not be undertaken unless the Church considered the matter really worthy of study.

The Bishop's statement read:

"If the events which took place in Fatima are true, and if they are claimed as supernatural, let us thank Our Lord who vouchsafed... to increase our faith and to correct our habits. If they are false, it is fitting that the falsity be discovered."

On April 14, 1930, the investigations were completed. And on October 13th of that year, just thirteen years after the Miracle of the Sun, the long-awaited decision of the Church was given.

It declared the visions of the children at Fatima worthy of belief and officially sanctioned religious devotions at the place where the Miracle of the Sun occurred.

In a few words this simple, long-awaited letter—culminating thirteen years of investigations, and literally thousands of pages of transcribed testimony—contained all the essential arguments for belief in the "Miracle":

"The solar phenomenon on the thirteenth of October, 1917, described in the press of the time, was most marvelous and caused the greatest impression on those who had the happiness of witnessing it.

"The children appointed beforehand the day and hour when it would happen. The news spread swiftly through all of Portugal and although the weather was inclement, with copious rain, thousands upon thousands of people assembled there and, at the time of the last apparition, saw all the manifestations of the sun as though it were paying homage to the Queen of Heaven and Earth, who was more brilliant than the sun (Canticles VI, 9).

"This phenomenon, which no astronomical observatory registered and which therefore was not natural, was witnessed by persons of all categories and of all social classes, believers and unbelievers, journalists of the principal Portuguese newspapers, and even by persons some miles away. Facts which annul any explanation of collective illusion."

Science would say only that there was no natural explanation. Spiritual authority alone could determine whether or not it might be supernatural.

The absolute materialist, who does not believe in God, may still say that the phenomenon was natural even though science cannot explain it. But this would not be reasonable in view of the fact that three ignorant children predicted the event which science cannot explain.

But then, absolute materialists are not reasonable men, however much they pretend to be. They are men of extreme prejudice, whose reason demands limits to what can be seen and measured if it has to do with the spiritual order (which imposes moral law) but who *in daily life accept things they cannot see or measure on a completely material plane.*

However, even most materialists are impressed when the Church passes judgment. They know that enemies of the

Aerial view of the Cova in 1951. See page 103 for diagram.

Locations of our witnesses in the Cova during the miracle

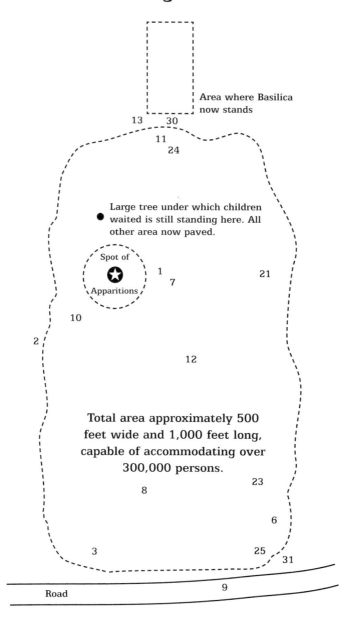

Area where Basilica now stands

13   30

11

24

Large tree under which children waited is still standing here. All other area now paved.

Spot of

Apparitions

1

7

21

10

2

12

Total area approximately 500 feet wide and 1,000 feet long, capable of accommodating over 300,000 persons.

23

8

6

3

25

31

Road   9

See aerial photo on page 101.

Witnesses are numbered in order of appearance in text.
Note:
★ marks those at spot of apparitions (within first circle).
○ marks those within larger area around spot of apparitions indicated on map by dotted circle. Others are located by their numbers:

1. Dominic Reis
2. Arturo dos Santos *
3. Dr. José Garrett *
4. Maria Teresa of Chainca °
5. Carlos Mendes °
6. Maria Celeste da Camara e Vasconcelos
7. José Joaquim da Assuncao
8. Higino Faria
9. Mario Godinho
10. Dona Maria Teresa Charters
11. Augusto Pereira dos Reis
12. Antonio Antunes de Oliveira
13. Manuel Francisco
14. Antonio dos Reis Novo ★

15. Joao Carreira ★
16. Maria do Carmo Menezes★
17. Maria dos Prazeres ★
18. José Joaquim da Silva ★
19. Joaquim da Silva Jorge ★
20. Antonio Rosa °
21. Joseph Frazao °
22. Antonio da Silva Reis °
23. Maria Guerra
24. Maria Candida da Silva °
25. Manuel Antonio Rainho *
26. Maria José Monteiro °
27. Julio Vicente ★
28. Joaquim Vicente *
29. Manuel da Silva °
30. Antonio Marques
31. Rev. Joao Manitra
32. Rev. Manuel Pereira da Silva
33. Rev. Manuel Formigao

---

*This location estimated since it does not appear precisely in testimony.

Church would merely need to prove that the Miracle did not take place to deal a terrible blow to the credibility of the world's largest Christian body.

The Catholic Church is two thousand years old and extremely slow to make a judgment on anything which affects the good of souls. It expects to be in the world until the end of time as the "deposit of truth." And though certain events may appear at any moment to be of major importance, the Church knows that all such great things of the moment will surely pass away and that only the basic, eternal truths remain.

Now, does ecclesiastical approval of Fatima mean that members of the Church must believe in this Miracle? The answer, of course, is no.

There are relatively few things which all Catholics must believe (these are the essential, basic truths of faith and morality). But often in this encyclopedic age the teaching authority

Immense crowds began to gather at Fatima following the approbation by the Church.

The Coronation: May 13, 1946.

of the Church gives guidance, especially when it would be extremely difficult—if not impossible—for individuals to reach a decision without the aid of such an authority. And the Miracle of Fatima falls into this latter, broad category.

Some ask why the decision of the "Church" in an event like that at Fatima should not have come from Rome rather than from the local Bishop.

The answer, very simply, is that it is proper that the Bishop of the place should issue the required proclamation.

Rome manifests its approval in other ways. In the case of Fatima, it has been manifested by Papal Legates sent to Fatima on two different occasions (a Papal Legate is a direct and personal representative of the Pope); by personal statements made by the Popes, and by action which has extended the cult of Fatima to the entire world.

Actually, Pope Pius XI outwardly showed belief in the message of Fatima before the Bishop of Fatima did so. In 1927 His Holiness distributed some pictures of Our Lady of Fatima to

Closing the Marian Year in 1954, Pope Pius XII crowned the centuries-old image from Saint Mary Major, recalling that: "We first crowned Our Lady as Queen of the World at Fatima."

students in Rome. And the first Portuguese Bishop (other than the Bishop of Fatima) who visited the place of the apparitions did so because he was influenced by Pope Pius XI. His successor, Pope Pius XII, had the message of Fatima emphasized throughout his pontificate.

During a general audience with Pope Pius XII, someone cried out: "Long live the Pope of Fatima!" There was an awkward moment of silence, and then the Holy Father smiled in the direction of the man who had cried out and said: *"Indeed, that is what I am."*

On numerous occasions the "Pope of Fatima" showed not only a great interest in the message, but a desire to attract to Fatima the attention of all the world. A few outstanding examples:

On October 1st, 1942, when acceding to the request of Our Lady of Fatima for a consecration of Russia to the Immaculate Heart of Mary, His Holiness made the consecration (of the world, including special reference to Russia) using the very language (Portuguese) in which the apparitions spoke.

In May, 1946, the Pontiff sent a Cardinal Legate *a latere* (a personal representative) to crown an image at the place of the apparitions. Speaking by short wave radio to the world as the Cardinal Legate placed the crown, the Holy Father proclaimed Our Lady of Fatima *Queen of the Universe.*

On October 13, 1951, again through a personal Cardinal legate, the Holy Father... at Fatima... closed the Holy Year for the entire world.

Another major event came in 1954 when the official Bull instituting the Feast of the Queenship of Mary recalled that the Holy Father "first crowned Our Lady 'Queen of the World' at Fatima."

However, to emphasize completely how the Church accepted the Miracle of the Sun would require many chapters.

The simple fact is: The proper Ecclesiastical authority proclaimed that what those hundred thousand persons saw on

October 13, 1917, at Fatima, was not natural and was to be attributed to God.

Chapter 17
WHAT DID IT PROVE?

Asked why they thought the Miracle occurred, all witnesses gave a similar answer:

"So that we might believe."

If we accept this as caused by God, then we must accept two corollaries: (1) The reality of the children's apparitions, and (2) The authenticity of the message.

Apparitions, as such, are not uncommon. And on examination we find that the apparitions of Fatima *in themselves* were never referred to by the children as particularly significant. In all six apparitions no special significance was attached to the *appearance* of the apparition. The apparition wore a brilliant star at the hem of the robe and a golden globe suspended around the neck. Yet no explanation was given of the globe and the star.

There is reason to believe that the globe represented the world, and that the star represented the red star of Russia which the apparition had promised to change into a star of light if certain conditions are fulfilled.

But again this is something we only can conjecture from the *message*.

So we conclude that the apparition, as such, was of secondary importance and that the Miracle was primarily wrought *to prove the message* brought by the apparitions to the world.

In summary, that message is this:

1. There is a heaven and an eternal state of separation from God, and at the present time "Many, many souls" are going to hell because "there is no one to pray and to make sacrifices for them;"

2. World War I was going to end but a second world war would begin within the reign of the next Pope (Pius XI). The world would know this second and more terrible war was about to begin when a strange light appeared in

the sky (This light appeared on January 17, 1939, and caused consternation throughout Europe; three months later Hitler marched into Austria);

3. Error will spread from Russia, through atheists, *fomenting further war;*
4. The Pope will suffer much;
5. The good will be persecuted;
6. Several nations will be annihilated;

However, (and this seems to be the most important part of the message)

7. *The above occurrences will take place only if this message is not heeded by the world and, in particular, if a sufficient number of persons do not cease offending God, already so much offended;*
8. If men do heed this message, the Vision promises: *"Russia will be converted, and there will be peace."*

In 1946, when this writer spent four consecutive hours with the eldest of the three children who carried on the conversations with the apparitions, most of the time was in discussion of this one subject: *Exactly what the vision wanted to prove to the world.*

She summarized it in that one sentence:

"Men must cease to offend God who is already so much offended."

Sometime after the Miracle was over, one of the children said to another:

"What are the sins by which men offend God?"

"I really don't know," the other child answered. "Missing Mass, I guess. Stealing, swearing, cursing..."

"And just for these things a soul goes to Hell?"

"Well... *it's a sin.*"

It is precisely here that world-conscience needs awakening.

The evil of sin is not so much in the act itself as in the fact that it is an *offense against God.*

Indeed, under some circumstances certain acts are not sinful, while under other circumstances they are. The evil of sin (which is the only true evil in the world) lies in the fact that it is *an offense against the Infinite Goodness of the Creator.*

This very simple, important fact is buried by modern man beneath an atmosphere of secularism.

The essential is our *relationship to God*. It is the same today as it was when Moses came down from Mount Sinai. It is the same today as when Sodom and Gomorrha were annihilated (in what a Soviet scientist recently suggested to have been a nuclear blast).

Tiny man, on a tiny globe in a tiny solar system, looks out into all the vastness of the universe and says as he throws a red star rocket at the moon: "God does not exist!" And this is the supreme offense.

One-third of the nations of the world are now controlled by men who take children from their families and educate them to deny God. They are atheists who build armies such as man never dreamed possible, armed with weapons capable of destroying all life on the planet, and they have vowed to wipe out religion from the earth—like the first "Red Star" revolution in the tiny nation where the Miracle of the Sun occurred.

For us in the free world and for all those enslaved in the Red world, the Miracle speaks.

It recalls to us—like a new Sinai—that God exists and that man rejects Him not only in the absolute heresy of Communism, but *whenever he disobeys and neglects God.*

Modern man's problem is the inability to accept moral authority. He pushes his claim of freedom to the point of denying the "Giver of freedom," and he embraces the ridiculous heresy of making his own objectives the rule of morality.

So while the fullness of the message of Fatima can be understood and embraced only by persons of a certain degree of faith, the ultimate, great message of the miracle of Fatima is for all mankind, with the universal plea which all must hear: *"Men must cease offending God, Who is already so much offended."*

We would like to end on this note, but for the "good" persons—for those who sincerely try not to offend God—the message of Fatima has particular directions.

During the first five apparitions the Vision specified certain aids which men could use to help them overcome themselves, to help them rise from the offenses against God which now deliver the world to the precipice of atomic war.

These positive conditions have been formulated into a simple pledge which has subsequently been signed by more than twenty million persons in fifty-seven nations. Those who keep this pledge are called "The Blue Army"—an army of positive religious action in the face of the mass of sinfulness which, like an ugly and festering boil, has come to a head in the militant atheism of a small party dictatorship in Russia.

This pledge of the Blue Army (which is a positive expression of the message of Fatima) contains only four directions:

1. A positive act of dedication to God, as in the wearing of a religious sign to remind ourselves, and to affirm that we belong to God;

2. A specific amount of daily prayer, considering a mystery of faith aimed at betterment of one's life;

3. An offering each morning of all thoughts and actions of one's entire day in reparation for sin and for the conversion of sinners;

4. Taking time once a month, (precisely on a certain day and precisely for five consecutive months) to renew one's purpose, to make a Communion of reparation, and to spend at least fifteen minutes in meditation upon an essential mystery of faith.

None of the above four acts is difficult. They are essentially the giving of one's will to God.

Taking into consideration the wasted "good intentions" and often abstract and nebulous attitude toward religion common to so many of us, these acts of the will proposed in the Message of Fatima are *direct, concrete, specific*, so that they may be objects of a positive resolution which one can consciously fulfill, and on which one can easily measure compliance.

This book about the Miracle of the Sun is not the place to go into great detail on the specific message of Fatima. Let it be sufficient to say here that the positive side of the message of the apparitions of Fatima is contained in the pledge of the Blue Army, which exists all over the world. Free literature is available from national centers in almost every nation.

The "Blue Army Pledge" was prepared in consultation with Lucia, who spoke to Our Lady. It was confirmed as complete and correct by the Bishop of Fatima, and promoted by him. It has been accepted throughout the world and has become the basis of world-wide effort to fulfill the message of the apparitions of Fatima.

Therefore, for those who want to be sure that they are carrying out the message of Fatima, they need only to make and keep the Blue Army pledge. And if they want to be sure that

His Eminence, Eugene Cardinal Tisserant, addresses the International meeting of the Blue Army in Vatican Pavilion of Brussels Fair, July, 1958. Next to the Cardinal is the Most Reverend John Venancio, Bishop of Fatima, and at extreme right is John Haffert, author of this book.

they are effectively causing the message of Fatima to be fulfilled by others in the world, they need merely see that this pledge is made by others, even as they keep it themselves.

But for all men, the message of the apparitions to the world is that men must cease to offend God. A simple formula of action is given, with the assurance that: "Russia will be converted and an era of peace conceded to all mankind."

Our greatest danger to success in obtaining fulfillment of this glorious promise of Fatima is probably not the atheists (who are rather objects of the promise than persons expected to fulfill its conditions).

Perhaps our greatest danger lies in our own failure to accept such a simple solution to the world's problems, and to accept the message of Fatima for what it is.

Chapter 18
FEAR AND HOPE

"The miracle never set too well with me," a businessman in a metropolitan suburb in America recently wrote. "It was too dramatic, too 'Madison Avenue,' if you will. It terrified people, and certainly this does not seem consistent with Love and Mercy. Besides it was the type of miracle that could be easily attributed to mass hysteria."

This objector then goes on to say that after worrying about this for years, his eyes widened when he read President Truman's announcement of the bomb which had been dropped on Hiroshima: "Man has learned," the President announced, "to produce the power of the sun here on earth."

The objecting American businessman suddenly asked himself:

"Twenty-eight years before, in the Miracle of the Sun, was God trying to tell us that man would soon learn how to harness the sun's power on earth for good or for evil... and that as the terrified crowd thought the world was about to end, so indeed it might if we did not wake up to Truths more vast than the atom?"

Like this thoughtful businessman perhaps there are many persons who at first do not *like* the "Miracle of the Sun" because it offends their conservatism. It seems disconsonant with the Majesty of God, as though it were an almost frantic attempt to get the attention of men. Added to the Miracle itself is the attention—getting device of the "1960 Secret" and someone said, perhaps not thinking of being sacrilegious, "How corny can you get?"

We may feel like rebelling against the *superlatives* which the message contains or implies: "*Most* of those who die in the great war will be lost" (Jacinta); "Several nations will be *annihilated*;" "Error will spread from an atheist Russia through the *entire world*" (part of July 13th prophecy).

Thus a natural and wholesome conservatism in religious matters may become a block to reception of the Fatima phenomena.

Conservatism has taken on the nature of a cardinal virtue in some who consider it of "essence" in the ageless role of the Church, already two thousand years alive and destined to bear its responsibilities until the end of time. And while they may be willing to accept the judgment of the Church on the authenticity of Fatima, they are reluctant to "follow through" with all that this acceptance implies.

If asked whether they believe in Fatima, they will be quick to affirm that they do. But they would prefer that we not talk of it, and that particularly we should not become too specific either about the miracle or the message. They are even a little horrified at an expression that Bishop Sheen used to describe Fatima: "Apocalyptic."

The message of Fatima, one must admit, *is not* conservative.* And if it has even *similar* antecedents in history, they are all pretty frightening.

Paul Claudel called the Miracle of the Sun "an explosion of the supernatural" and to the most conservative it may appear as a slightly dangerous explosion.

This miracle touches problems such as world fear and emphasis on secondary aids to Sanctity. Indeed, one cannot help but admire those conservative churchmen who—despite this—accept and promote the message of Fatima with humble faith.

Many seem to feel that the Church was slow in passing judgment on the Miracle of Fatima, but it is remarkable that the Church moved so quickly. It was only ten years after the Miracle of the Sun that Pope Pius XI encouraged belief in Fatima; only thirteen years before the "official" approval was

---

(*) Editor's note: *Meet the Witnesses* was written forty-five years ago and, most unfortunately, its devoted author is now deceased. While even today we carefully distinguish between social, fiscal, and foreign policy conservatives, one can say that conservative Catholics today are entirely open to the message of conversion that the Mother of God brought men, and constitute a major pillar of support for the Fatima apostolate.

given; and only twenty-five years before Pope Pius XII, in an international broadcast, drew the attention of the entire world to the Fatima message.

To get some idea of how relatively "speedy" this is, we need merely consider the fact that the *least time* required by the Church in modern history for canonization of a Saint (canonization of Saint Therese of Lisieux) was twenty-five years.

The great length of time required for a canonization is due to the fact that the Church wants to be *absolutely certain when sanctioning belief of all the faithful* even in something as apparently harmless as that some good person is truly in Heaven. And the processes involved in canonization would astound the layman. The reams of testimony, gathered over years, would normally greatly outweigh the evidence that is gathered and weighed in a criminal court where the life of an accused person might be at stake.

It is to be hoped that this book has helped the reader to grasp the shattering nature of this event.

There is nothing gentle about this explosion!

If we put ourselves in the places of the witnesses whom we have met: *How would it feel to be convinced, at this moment, that the world was about to end in ten minutes?*

The very children to whom the message of Fatima was given were told, two months before the Miracle, that if they did not deny their prophecies they would be boiled alive in oil. Then one by one, the children were taken out of jail, ostensibly to be tossed to a hideous death. Weeping, after two days of interrogation, they permitted themselves to be dragged forth, their faith so strong because of what they had seen that they preferred to die in this most repulsive and agonizing manner than to deny that a vision from Heaven had foretold a miracle *"So that everyone may believe."*

When the miracle did come, the fear and terror of the crowd was so great that many fainted. Afterward many momentarily could not remember where they were or even who they were. To this day, some who were alone in the surrounding area and therefore had no others around them to help bring them back to their senses, cannot remember anything just after the miracle.

People wept and groveled in the mud, cried their sins aloud, pleaded for mercy.

Again, can we imagine ourselves in that same position? Can you imagine yourself, in the presence of thousands of people, crying out your most secret sins?

Yet, this happened.

We may consider ourselves too brave to be affected by a miracle like this, but were not some of those tens of thousands of persons on the mountain brave? Yet very few of those witnesses will hesitate to admit, even after all these years, that *they were afraid.*

Yet, even in the same breath with which we speak of the terrible fear the Miracle caused in those who beheld it, so we must speak of something equally extreme and marvelous in the Miracle: *Hope.*

The crowd expected to be destroyed at that moment, but was suddenly spared. Even the discomfort experienced in the cold rain was suddenly lifted. They were exalted with a great joy of the "supernatural"—*the joy of believing that God is in His Heaven, and that all could be right in the world.*

If the message of Fatima is terrible, it is also filled with the greatest hope the atomic age could possibly have.

Where statesmen and scientists may see no solution to the atomic threat, the message of Fatima not only promises a solution, but even specifies what it will be:

"Russia will change."

Indeed, should all the most terrible things prophesied come to pass (which they need not, if people fulfill the requests specified in the message), we are promised that ultimately there will be peace.

Thus the Miracle of the Sun is rather an explosion of hope than of fear.

We are already afraid, because the atomic race is upon us. This message merely explains the *cause* of our fear. Then it offers hope if we will each cooperate to remove the cause of war (the ignoring of God and His Law).

We cannot be passive about this miracle. This is a great, a terrible, shattering intervention of the Divine while atomic war threatens the world.

How grave must be the threat of atheistic Communism! God, and only God, could have caused the miracle of Fatima. The message of Fatima is from Him. How can we ignore it? And at what risk?

A book about Fatima had been sent to Douglas Hyde, one of England's top communists, for criticism in the *Daily Worker.* He was going to throw it away, "Because it dealt with the supernatural, and I did not believe in the supernatural." But on an impulse, after his day's work, he tucked the book about Fatima under his arm and took it home... the same home which housed the most complete Marxist library in Great Britain. He read it, and reasoned that either the story was true or the

Douglas Hyde, formerly one of England's top communists, as he appeared speaking at the Peace Congress in Lisbon, October 12, 1951.

Church was monstrously foolish. This began investigations which led him to God. The day he resigned from the *Daily Worker* (as also happened in the case of Budenz in New York) the Communist party was so taken by surprise that Hyde's name still appeared as editor on the masthead of the edition which denounced him for leaving the Party.

Another book could be written... by men like Hamish Frazer, Douglas Hyde, Louis Budenz... *on the effect of the Miracle of the Sun outside of Portugal.*

In the United States the Blue Army produces a television program on which has appeared: the now President Kennedy (who appeared while Senator of Massachusetts), General Gruenther (formerly head of NATO forces and then President of the American Red Cross), Alfred Luns (Foreign Secretary of the Netherlands and President of NATO), Doctor Malik (who appeared while President of the General Assembly of the United Nations), Henry Cabot Lodge (who appeared while United States Ambassador to the U.N.), outstanding members of the United States Senate and House of Representatives, and experts from many other fields.

Each of these believes in what the program tries to say: That the struggle against Communism is basically a *spiritual struggle;* while the free world... if it is to survive... must maintain a deterrent military strength, it must above all *deepen it's moral convictions.*

The Blue Army televises celebrities, illustrating their words with films exposing the brutal nature of Communist aggression. But this television series speaks very little of Fatima as such.

"The world is not tuned to believe in miracles," said Monsignor Colgan, Founder of the Blue Army. "Among believers, the miracle of Fatima may create militancy in the cold war; among nonbelievers it usually creates only confused wonder."

Therefore the Blue Army television program deals directly

with the *nature* of Communism... Godless, bestial, recognizing
no law outside of itself... the "absolute heresy." It emphasizes
that the choice in the world today is between believing in God
and not believing. The Communists say that those who cannot
be vanquished must be destroyed. Siberia and firing squads
have become their ultimate alternate to atheism.

*There is a choice to be made, at this crucial moment of his-
tory, by each of us.* If we lose this struggle... in which the annihilation of whole nations is at stake... it will be because we
remained "neutral," because we stood on the sidelines and
wondered about it all. Were we shocked to see China fall to
Communism? Were we perhaps even more shocked to see
Cuba, so close to the mainland of the United States itself,
become a Soviet base? Yet, shocked though we have been by
Communist expansion... *what have we done?* Have we said
any extra prayers? Have we realized that this struggle was a
spiritual one... with the enemy bending its primary attack on
God Himself? Have we made any reparations? *Have we
stopped being neutral and chosen sides?*

Let us choose now.